ASIS Thesaurus
of
Information Science and
Librarianship

ASIS Thesaurus
of
Information Science and
Librarianship

Jessica L. Milstead
Editor

ASIS Monograph Series

Published for the American Society for Information Science
by Learned Information, Inc.
Medford, NJ
1994

ISBN: 0-938734-80-6

Price: $34.95

Book Editor: James H. Shelton
Cover Design: M. Heide Dengler

Printed in the United States of America

Table of Contents

Introduction

This first edition of the *ASIS Thesaurus of Information Science and Librarianship* seeks to cover the fields of information science and librarianship. Related and peripheral fields are covered as warranted by the strength of their relationship to information science and librarianship. Among the related fields are computer science, linguistics, and behavioral and cognitive sciences. More limited coverage of peripheral fields such as education, economics, management, statistics, and sociology is also included.

The scope is limited primarily to topical subjects. Proper names of organizations, programs, etc., are excluded; the primary exceptions are the names of a few tools which are key to indexing and cataloging practice. There are 1312 descriptors, 680 Use references, and 37 facet indicators in the thesaurus.

The thesaurus is intended primarily as a resource to aid in indexing and searching in the fields of information science and librarianship. It is also intended to serve as a guide to the terminology of the fields for students and researchers.

The National Information Standards Organization *Guidelines for Construction, Format, and Maintenance of Monolingual Thesauri* were followed in compilation. Authorities in the field (listed below) were used as resources for terms. The Liu Palmer Thesaurus Construction System (TCS) Professional Edition software package, Version 1.3b, was used in compilation.

Guidelines for Use

The thesaurus includes preferred terms (descriptors) and nonpreferred terms (Use references). Scope notes provide information about the use of terms in the thesaurus, as well as definitions of ambiguous terms. Three ways of approaching the thesaurus are provided:

- An alphabetical display provides the full record for each descriptor, including its BT (Broader Term), NT (Narrower Term), RT (Related Term), and UF (Used For) references, as well as scope notes. This display also includes Use cross references from nonpreferred terms. A sample entry:

Descriptor →		journals	
	SN	Scholarly journals.	← *Scope note*
Used for reference →	UF	scholarly journals	
	BT	periodicals	← *Broader term reference*
Narrower term reference →	NT	electronic journals	
	RT	primary literature	← *Related term reference*
		scholarly publishing	↙

Nonpreferred term →	scholarly journals		
	USE	journals	← *Reference to descriptor*

- A hierarchical display shows each descriptor in its place(s) in the hierarchy of terms, based on BT/NT relationships. An example of part of the hierarchical display:

> (communications activities)
> . communications
> . . telecommunications
> . . . video communications
> . . . . television
> . . . . . cable television
> . . . . . HDTV
>
> (communications media)
> . audiotex
> . mass media
> . . newspapers*
> . . radio
> . . television*
> . multimedia
> . videotex

Descriptors followed by an asterisk (*) in the hierarchical display are polyhierarchical, i.e., they have more than one BT. One of the BT's of such terms is treated as "primary" by the software; all others, considered secondary, are designated by an asterisk. If a polyhierarchical term has NT's, these appear only under its primary occurrence. The NT's of a term which is followed by an asterisk may be determined by searching under the term in the alphabetical display. In the example above, "television" is polyhierarchical, and its NT appears only under its primary occurrence.

- A rotated (KWIC) display shows each descriptor arranged in alphabetical order by every word appearing in the term. An example from the rotated display:

```
               control systems
 bibliographic control
       quality control
    vocabulary control
        access control (computer systems)
```

The thesaurus has a faceted hierarchical structure. Facets are broad terms such as "(activities and operations)" or "(fields and disciplines)," not authorized for use in indexing, which are used to group related concepts together. These terms are always in parentheses; they appear in their hierarchical position in the hierarchical display, and where appropriate, as BT's to descriptors in the alphabetical display. They do not appear in the alphabetical display on their own. A hierarchical display of the facets used in the thesaurus is at the end of this introduction.

To accommodate the limitations of many present-day search systems, use of punctuation in the thesaurus is minimized. The hyphen is used only where necessary for clarity of a term; where it was feasible to combine a prefix with the following word, or substitute a space for the hyphen as a connector, this has been done. Examples are:

computer aided design
online
use-sensitive pricing

The apostrophe ("children's literature") has been retained. The only other punctuation marks to be found in descriptors are the parentheses, used to delimit explanatory qualifiers, e.g., "links (hypertext)" as well as to enclose facet terms.

In conformity with the thesaurus standard, written-out forms of terms are preferred to abbreviations or acronyms, with Use references made from the latter. An exception is made when a shortened form is used much more often than the written-out form, e.g., "OPACs," rather than "online public access catalogs."

Sources Used in Compilation

Aitchison, Jean. *Communication and Information Thesaurus*. English edition. The Hague: International Federation for Documentation; Paris: Unesco, 1992.

American Federation of Information Processing Societies. *Taxonomy of Computer Science and Engineering*. New York: AFIPS, 1980.

American Society for Information Science. Annual Meeting. *Proceedings*. Medford, NJ: Learned Information, Inc.

Annual Review of Information Science and Technology. Martha E. Williams, ed. Amsterdam: Elsevier Science Publishers; Medford, NJ: Learned Information, Inc.

Information Science Abstracts. New York: Plenum Publishing Corp. (Descriptor field of online database)

International Organization for Standardization. *Documentation and Information — Vocabulary — Part 1: Basic Concepts*. 1st ed. Switzerland: ISO, 1983. (ISO 5127/1-1983(E/F))

International Organization for Standardization. *Documentation and Information — Vocabulary — Part 2: Traditional Documents*. 1st ed. Switzerland: ISO, 1983. (ISO 5127/2-1983)

International Organization for Standardization. *Documentation and Information — Vocabulary — Part 6: Documentary Languages*. 1st ed. Switzerland: ISO, 1983. (ISO 5127/6-1983)

International Organization for Standardization. *Documentation and Information — Vocabulary — Section 3a): Acquisition, Identification, and Analysis of Documents and Data*. 1st ed. Switzerland: ISO, 1981. (ISO 5127/3a-1981)

Library Literature: 1992. New York: H.W. Wilson Co., 1993.

LISA Online User Manual. 2d ed. Oxford, England: Learned Information, 1987.

National Information Standards Organization. *Guidelines for Construction, Format, and Maintenance of Monolingual Thesauri*. Washington, DC: NISO. (In press) (Z39.19-199x).

Schultz, Claire K. *Thesaurus of Information Science Terminology*. Revised ed. Washington, DC: Communication Service Corp., 1968.

Watters, Carolyn. *Dictionary of Information Science and Technology*. New York: Academic Press, 1992.

Wersig, Gernot; Neveling, Ulrich. *Terminology of Documentation*. Paris: Unesco Press, 1976.

Acknowledgments

First and foremost, acknowledgments are due to the members of the Advisory Board, who read drafts, advised, and contributed greatly to the quality of the final product. They are:

Jean Aitchison
Harold Borko
Trudi Bellardo Hahn
Marie Kascus
Anne Meagher
Candy Schwartz
Debora Shaw
Jennifer Younger

Jean Aitchison, in particular, provided immense assistance in straightening out knotty problems with a number of the facets. While some of the facets draw very heavily on her contribution, any less-than-optimum features of the organization must be attributed to the author. Dr. Robert Fugmann also provided helpful comments. My assistant, Beverly Pajer, was vigilant to assure that errors did not creep into the work.

All these people contributed greatly to the thesaurus. Any errors and omissions, however, are the full responsibility of the author.

This is a first edition, and it is anticipated that it will be updated regularly. Suggestions for improvements are solicited, and should be directed to the author.

Jessica L. Milstead
The JELEM Company
P.O. Box 5063
Brookfield, CT 06804

Facet List

(activities and operations)
. (business and management operations)
. (communications activities)
. (computer operations)
. (educational and psychological activities)
. (general activities)
. (information and library operations)
. (socioeconomic activities)
. (technical and manufacturing operations)
(buildings and facilities)
(communications media)
(document types)
. (by availability, access, organization)
. (by information content, purpose)
. (by medium, physical form)
(fields and disciplines)
(hardware, equipment, and systems)
(knowledge, information, etc.)
. (by content)
. (information representations)
. (knowledge and information organization devices)
. (languages)
. (linguistic elements)
(natural functions and events)
(networks)
(organizations)
(persons and informal groups)
(physical media)
(product and service providers)
(qualities)
. (general qualities)
. (human qualities)
. (qualities of information and data)
. (qualities of systems and equipment)
(research and analytic methods)
(sectors of the economy)
(sociocultural aspects)

Alphabetical Display

AACR
    USE: Anglo American Cataloguing
        Rules
abbreviations
    BT: information representations
    RT: acronyms
aboutness
    BT: (qualities of information and
            data)
    RT: indexing
            information retrieval systems
abstract data types
    SN: Data structures with associated
            axioms defining the semantics of
            the operations.
    BT: data structures
    NT: objects (data structures)
abstracting
    BT: summarization
    NT: automatic abstracting
    RT: abstracting and indexing services
            abstracts
abstracting and indexing services
    UF: indexing services
            secondary information services
    BT: database producers
    RT: abstracting
            abstracts
            bibliographic databases
            current awareness services
            databases
            indexes (information retrieval)
            indexing
            information infrastructure
            periodical indexes
            value added
abstraction
    BT: mental processes
    RT: classification
            generalization
abstracts
    BT: document surrogates
    NT: author abstracts

abstracts (cont.)
    RT: abstracting
            abstracting and indexing services
            annotations
            databases
            digests
academic freedom
    BT: civil rights
    RT: censorship
            colleges and universities
            intellectual freedom
academic institutions
    USE: colleges and universities
academic libraries
    UF: college libraries
            university libraries
    BT: colleges and universities
            libraries
    NT: community college libraries
    RT: library networks
            research libraries
academic publishing
    USE: scholarly publishing
access control (computer systems)
    BT: computer security
access points
    SN: The terms by means of which
            access may be gained to the
            information in a file; in controlled
            vocabularies, both preferred and
            nonpreferred terms.
    BT: (knowledge and information
            organization devices)
    NT: entries
            entry vocabularies
            headings
            links (hypertext)
    RT: citation order
access to resources
    SN: Access to information and
            document resources.
    BT: (information and library
            operations)

access to resources (cont.)
    NT: bibliographic access
           document access
           information access
           library access
           remote access
access vocabularies
    USE: entry vocabularies
accounting
    BT: (business and management
          operations)
    NT: auditing
    RT: financial management
accreditation
    BT: (educational and psychological
          activities)
    RT: education
          evaluation
accuracy
    BT: (general qualities)
    RT: currency (in time)
          data corruption
          error correction
          error detection
          error rates
          errors
          usability
acoustics
    USE: sound
acquisitions (of materials)
    UF: library acquisitions
    BT: collection development
    NT: approval plans
          claiming (acquisitions)
          gifts and exchanges
          ordering (materials)
          subscriptions
acronyms
    UF: initialisms
    BT: information representations
    RT: abbreviations
adjacency searching
    USE: proximity searching
administration
    USE: management

administrative records
    BT: records
admissibility of records
    SN: Admissibility in the legal process.
    BT: legal aspects
adolescent literature
    USE: young adult literature
ADP
    USE: data processing
adult education
    BT: education
    RT: basic education
          continuing education
          lifelong learning
          off campus education
adult literacy
    USE: literacy
adult programs
    USE: library programs
advertising
    BT: marketing
aerospace
    BT: (fields and disciplines)
agency cooperation
    USE: cooperation
aging of literatures
    SN: Aging of information content.
    BT: (qualities of information and
          data)
    RT: obsolescence
aging of materials
    SN: Physical aging.
    BT: (natural functions and events)
    RT: information life cycle
algorithms
    BT: (by content)
    RT: computer software
almanacs
    BT: reference materials
alphabetical arrangement
    UF: alphabetical order
          alphabetization
    BT: arrangement
    NT: letter by letter arrangement
          word by word arrangement
    RT: sort sequences

alphabetical order
    USE: alphabetical arrangement
alphabetico classed indexes
    BT: indexes (information retrieval)
alphabetization
    USE: alphabetical arrangement
alphabets
    BT: writing systems
alternative materials
    USE: alternative publications
alternative publications
    UF: alternative materials
          fugitive materials
          underground publications
    BT: publications
    RT: grey literature
          small presses
ambiguity
    BT: (qualities of information and
          data)
    RT: disambiguation
          uncertainty
analog data
    BT: data
analog systems
    BT: computer systems
analog to digital conversion
    USE: digitization
analogies
    USE: metaphors
analysis of variance
    UF: ANOVA
    BT: statistical methods
analytical bibliography
    UF: descriptive bibliography
          historical bibliography
    BT: bibliography
anaphora
    BT: information representations
    RT: syntactics
Anglo American Cataloguing Rules
    UF: AACR
    BT: cataloging rules
    RT: cataloging (bibliographic)

animation
    BT: (computer operations)
    RT: computer graphics
annotations
    BT: document surrogates
    RT: abstracts
ANOVA
    USE: analysis of variance
answer passage retrieval
    UF: question answering retrieval
    BT: information retrieval
    RT: fact retrieval systems
anthropology
    BT: behavioral sciences
          social sciences
antiquarian materials
    USE: rare materials
antonymy
    BT: semantic relationships
approval ordering
    USE: approval plans
approval plans
    UF: approval ordering
    BT: acquisitions (of materials)
architecture
    SN: Of structures, not of computers,
          for which see "computer
          architecture."
    BT: (fields and disciplines)
    RT: buildings
          fine arts
archival storage
    UF: backup storage
    BT: computer storage
    RT: archives
archives
    UF: historical records
    BT: (product and service providers)
    RT: archival storage
          genealogy
          libraries
          manuscripts
          rare materials
          records management
archivists
    BT: information professionals

area studies
    BT: (fields and disciplines)
    RT: social sciences
armed forces
    BT: organizations
arrangement
    UF: filing
    BT: (information and library
          operations)
    NT: alphabetical arrangement
          systematic arrangement
    RT: classification
          sort sequences
array processors
    BT: processing units (computers)
art
    BT: fine arts
    RT: image information systems
          images
          visual materials
articles, periodical
    USE: periodical articles
artificial intelligence
    BT: computer software
    NT: computer vision
          expert systems
          machine learning
          natural language processing
          neural networks
    RT: cybernetics
          intelligent interfaces
          knowledge bases
assessment, needs
    USE: needs assessment
assignment indexing
    BT: indexing
    RT: vocabulary control
associations
    USE: professional associations
associative memory
    BT: memory (computer)
    RT: associative retrieval
associative processing
    USE: associative retrieval

associative relationships
    UF: nonhierarchical relationships
          related term relationships
          RT relationships
    BT: semantic relationships
    RT: cross references
associative retrieval
    UF: associative processing
    BT: information retrieval
    RT: associative memory
          probabilistic indexing
          probabilistic retrieval
attitudes
    BT: psychological aspects
    RT: human behavior
audio cassettes
    USE: audiocassettes
audio communications
    BT: telecommunications
audio interfaces
    UF: voice input
    BT: human computer interfaces
    RT: speech recognition
          speech synthesis
audio recordings
    USE: sound recordings
audio tapes
    USE: audiotapes
audio-visual materials
    USE: nonprint media
audiocassettes
    UF: audio cassettes
          audiotape cassettes
          cassettes, audiotape
    BT: audiotapes
    RT: cassette recorders
audiodisk recordings
    USE: sound recordings
audiotape cassettes
    USE: audiocassettes
audiotapes
    UF: audio tapes
    BT: magnetic tapes
          sound recordings
    NT: audiocassettes
          digital audio tapes

audiotex
    BT: (communications media)
audiovisual aids
    USE: nonprint media
audiovisual materials
    USE: nonprint media
auditing
    BT: accounting
author abstracts
    BT: abstracts
author indexes
    SN: Indexes to authors; for indexes
          prepared by authors of the works
          involved, use "author-prepared
          indexes."
    BT: indexes (information retrieval)
author-prepared indexes
    BT: indexes (information rctrieval)
authoring (hypermedia)
    SN: For writing of linear texts, use
          "authorship."
    BT: (computer operations)
    RT: hypermedia
          hypertext
authority files
    BT: files
    RT: cataloging (bibliographic)
          controlled vocabularies
          entries
          indexing
          personal names
          proper names
authors
    UF: writers
    BT: (persons and informal groups)
    NT: coauthors
authorship
    SN: Of linear texts. For preparation
          of hypermedia use "authoring."
    UF: coauthorship
          writing
    BT: communications
    NT: technical writing
automata
    BT: (research and analytic methods)

automatic abstracting
    BT: abstracting
    RT: automatic extracting
automatic classification
    BT: classification
    RT: automatic indexing
          cluster analysis
automatic data processing
    USE: data processing
automatic extracting
    BT: extracting
    RT: automatic abstracting
automatic indexing
    BT: indexing
    RT: automatic classification
          computational linguistics
          information processing
          knowledge bases
          natural language processing
automatic translation
    USE: machine translation
automatic...
    UF: computerized ...
    BT: (computer operations)
automation
    SN: Automation or computerization as
          an issue; for particular
          applications, use the name of the
          application, e.g., automatic
          indexing.
    BT: (computer operations)
    NT: library automation
          office automation
availability of information
    USE: information access
back end processors
    SN: Equipment which processes data
          in response to a query presented
          at a host processor, before any
          data are actually transferred to
          the host.
    BT: processing units (computers)
back of book indexes
    USE: book indexes
back of book indexing
    USE: book indexing

backup storage
  USE: archival storage
banned materials
  UF: censored materials
  BT: (by availability, access,
        organization)
  RT: censorship
        freedom to read
        intellectual freedom
        library materials
bar codes
  BT: information representations
  RT: optical recognition
basic education
  SN: Fundamental education that is
        basic to later learning.
  BT: education
  RT: adult education
batch processing
  BT: data processing
baud rate
  USE: transmission speed
Bayesian functions
  UF: Bayesian systems
        Bayesian theory
  BT: statistical methods
  RT: probability
Bayesian systems
  USE: Bayesian functions
Bayesian theory
  USE: Bayesian functions
BBS
  USE: bulletin board systems
behavior, human
  USE: human behavior
behavioral sciences
  BT: (fields and disciplines)
  NT: anthropology
        psychology
        sociology
  RT: social sciences
benchmarks
  BT: evaluation
  RT: standardization
        standards

bibliographic access
  BT: access to resources
  RT: document access
        information access
bibliographic citations
  UF: citations, bibliographic
  BT: bibliographic records
  RT: citation searching
bibliographic control
  BT: (information and library
        operations)
  RT: bibliographies
        bibliography
        cataloging (bibliographic)
bibliographic coupling
  UF: coupling, bibliographic
  BT: citation analysis
  RT: citation indexes
        cocitation analysis
bibliographic data
  USE: bibliographic records
bibliographic databases
  BT: databases
  NT: full text databases
        OPACs
  RT: abstracting and indexing services
        bibliographies
        indexes (information retrieval)
        reference retrieval systems
bibliographic description
  USE: descriptive cataloging
bibliographic instruction
  UF: library instruction
        media instruction
        use instruction
  BT: training
  RT: information literacy
        library skills
        user training
        users
bibliographic records
  UF: bibliographic data
        catalog records
  BT: document surrogates
        records

bibliographic records (cont.)
- NT: bibliographic citations
- MARC records

bibliographic retrieval systems
- USE: reference retrieval systems

bibliographic utilities
- UF: host computers
- BT: (product and service providers)
- RT: information utilities

bibliographies
- BT: (by information content, purpose)
- NT: national bibliographies
- RT: bibliographic control
- bibliographic databases
- bibliography
- indexes (information retrieval)

bibliography
- BT: (information and library operations)
- NT: analytical bibliography
- RT: bibliographic control
- bibliographies

bibliometrics
- UF: co-word analysis
- BT: infometrics
- NT: Bradford's law
- citation analysis
- Lotka's law
- RT: growth
- information use
- scatter (bibliometrics)

bibliotherapy
- BT: (educational and psychological activities)
- RT: reading

bilingualism
- BT: (sociocultural aspects)

binderies
- UF: binders
- bookbinders
- BT: (product and service providers)
- RT: binding

binders
- USE: binderies

binding
- UF: book binding
- bookbinding
- BT: preservation of library materials
- RT: binderies
- technical services (libraries)

biology
- BT: biomedical sciences

biomedical sciences
- UF: health sciences
- BT: natural sciences
- NT: biology
- medicine
- pharmacology
- RT: genomes
- physicians

bit-mapped images
- BT: images

blanket orders
- BT: ordering (materials)

blind persons
- USE: disabled persons

book binding
- USE: binding

book collecting
- BT: (information and library operations)

book collections
- USE: library collections

book indexes
- SN: Indexes to individual books, not indexes in book form.
- UF: back of book indexes
- BT: indexes (information retrieval)

book indexing
- UF: back of book indexing
- BT: indexing

book reviews
- UF: literary reviews
- reviews, book
- BT: reviews

book stock
- USE: library collections

book trade
- USE: book vendors

book vendors
 UF: book trade
     booksellers
 BT: vendors
bookbinders
 USE: binderies
bookbinding
 USE: binding
bookmobiles
 BT: mobile libraries
books
 BT: (by medium, physical form)
     publications
 NT: paperbacks
     talking books
     textbooks
 RT: fiction
     large print materials
     monographs
     nonfiction
     standard book numbers
booksellers
 USE: book vendors
Boolean functions
 USE: Boolean logic
Boolean logic
 UF: Boolean functions
     logical operators
     operators, logical
 BT: logic
 RT: Boolean searching
Boolean searching
 UF: Boolean strategies
 BT: searching
 RT: Boolean logic
Boolean strategies
 USE: Boolean searching
borrowers
 USE: library users
borrowing
 USE: circulation (library)
Bradford's law
 BT: bibliometrics
 RT: core literature
     scatter (bibliometrics)

Braille
 BT: writing systems
branch libraries
 BT: libraries
 RT: public libraries
bridge agents
 USE: gatekeepers
broadband transmission
 BT: data transmission
broadcasting
 BT: telecommunications
 RT: radio
     television
broader term references
 USE: cross references
broader term relationships
 USE: hierarchical relationships
browsing
 BT: searching
 RT: serendipity
BT references
 USE: cross references
BT relationships
 USE: hierarchical relationships
budgeting
 BT: financial management
buildings
 BT: (buildings and facilities)
 NT: library buildings
 RT: architecture
bulletin board systems
 UF: BBS
     electronic bulletin boards
 BT: message systems
business
 UF: industry
 BT: (business and management
     operations)
cable television
 BT: television
CAD
 USE: computer aided design
CAE
 USE: computer aided engineering
CAI
 USE: computer assisted instruction

CAM
    USE: computer aided manufacturing
cameras
    BT: (hardware, equipment, and
           systems)
candidate descriptors
    SN: Terms proposed for addition to a
           controlled vocabulary.
    BT: index terms
    RT: thesauri
card catalogs
    BT: catalogs (bibliographic)
cartography
    UF: mapping (cartography)
    BT: (fields and disciplines)
    RT: maps
CASE
    USE: computer aided software
           engineering
case grammar
    BT: grammars
case histories
    USE: case studies
case studies
    UF: case histories
    BT: (research and analytic methods)
cassette recorders
    BT: tape recorders
    NT: videocassette recorders
    RT: audiocassettes
cassettes, audiotape
    USE: audiocassettes
catalog entries
    USE: entries
catalog records
    USE: bibliographic records
cataloging (bibliographic)
    BT: organization of information
           technical services (libraries)
    NT: cataloging in publication
           computerized cataloging
           descriptive cataloging
           minimal cataloging
           retrospective cataloging
           shared cataloging

cataloging (bibliographic) (cont.)
    RT: Anglo American Cataloguing
           Rules
           authority files
           bibliographic control
           catalogs (bibliographic)
cataloging in publication
    UF: CIP
    BT: cataloging (bibliographic)
cataloging rules
    BT: (knowledge and information
           organization devices)
    NT: Anglo American Cataloguing
           Rules
catalogs (bibliographic)
    BT: (by information content, purpose)
    NT: card catalogs
           classified catalogs
           OPACs
           union catalogs
    RT: cataloging (bibliographic)
           indexes (information retrieval)
categories
    BT: (knowledge and information
           organization devices)
    RT: semantic relationships
cathode ray tube terminals
    USE: video display terminals
CD (compact disks)
    USE: compact discs
CD-I
    USE: compact disc interactive
CD-ROM
    UF: compact disc read only memory
    BT: compact discs
    RT: CD-ROM drives
           compact disc interactive
           digital video interactive
CD-ROM drives
    BT: disk drives
    NT: jukeboxes
    RT: CD-ROM
cellular communications
    UF: cellular telephones
           mobile telephones
    BT: mobile communications

cellular telephones
　　USE: cellular communications
censored materials
　　USE: banned materials
censorship
　　BT:　(sociocultural aspects)
　　RT:　academic freedom
　　　　　banned materials
　　　　　freedom of information
　　　　　freedom to read
　　　　　intellectual freedom
central libraries
　　UF:　main libraries
　　BT:　libraries
central processing units
　　USE: processing units (computers)
centralization
　　BT:　(business and management
　　　　　operations)
　　RT:　decentralization
chain indexing
　　BT:　subject indexing
　　RT:　citation order
change
　　BT:　(sociocultural aspects)
　　RT:　growth
character recognition
　　USE: optical character recognition
character sets
　　BT:　information representations
　　RT:　diacriticals
　　　　　legibility
charges
　　USE: pricing
charging systems
　　USE: circulation (library)
chemical information
　　BT:　scientific and technical
　　　　　information
　　NT:　chemical nomenclature
　　　　　chemical structures
　　　　　connection tables (chemistry)
chemical nomenclature
　　BT:　chemical information
　　　　　terminology

chemical structures
　　BT:　chemical information
　　　　　information representations
chemistry
　　BT:　physical sciences
　　RT:　pharmacology
children's books
　　USE: children's literature
children's librarianship
　　USE: children's services
children's libraries
　　BT:　libraries
children's literature
　　UF:　children's books
　　BT:　(by information content, purpose)
children's services
　　UF:　children's librarianship
　　BT:　library services
　　RT:　storytelling
CIM
　　USE: computer integrated
　　　　　manufacturing
CIP
　　USE: cataloging in publication
circulation (library)
　　UF:　borrowing
　　　　　charging systems
　　　　　lending
　　　　　loans
　　BT:　technical services (libraries)
　　RT:　overdue materials
　　　　　reader services
citation analysis
　　BT:　bibliometrics
　　NT:　bibliographic coupling
　　　　　cocitation analysis
citation indexes
　　BT:　indexes (information retrieval)
　　RT:　bibliographic coupling
　　　　　citation searching
citation order
　　SN:　The order in which elements are
　　　　　listed in an index entry; used
　　　　　particularly with regard to chain
　　　　　indexing.

citation order (cont.)
- UF: facet formula
  - preferred order
- BT: (qualities of information and data)
- RT: access points
  - chain indexing
  - faceted classification
  - index terms

citation searching
- SN: Searching for documents that have cited a known document.
- BT: searching
- RT: bibliographic citations
  - citation indexes

citations, bibliographic
- USE: bibliographic citations

civil rights
- BT: (sociocultural aspects)
- NT: academic freedom
  - intellectual freedom
  - privacy

claiming (acquisitions)
- BT: acquisitions (of materials)
- RT: subscriptions

classification
- SN: Theory of classification. For particular schemes, use "classification schemes."
- UF: classified arrangement
- BT: organization of information
- NT: automatic classification
  - faceted classification
  - hierarchical classification
  - notation synthesis
  - taxonomy
- RT: abstraction
  - arrangement
  - classification schemes
  - classified catalogs
  - index terms
  - indexing
  - knowledge representation
  - notation
  - systematic arrangement

classification construction
- USE: index language construction

classification schemes
- UF: taxonomies
- BT: index languages
- NT: Dewey Decimal Classification
  - International Patent Classification
  - Library of Congress Classification
  - Universal Decimal Classification
- RT: classification
  - classified catalogs
  - controlled vocabularies
  - index language construction
  - indexing
  - notation
  - thesaurofacet

classified arrangement
- USE: systematic arrangement

classified arrangement
- USE: classification

classified catalogs
- BT: catalogs (bibliographic)
- RT: classification
  - classification schemes

clearinghouses (community information)
- USE: community information services

clearinghouses (information analysis)
- USE: information analysis centers

clearinghouses (special libraries)
- USE: special libraries

client server systems
- UF: host computers
- BT: computer systems
- RT: file servers

cliometrics
- USE: infometrics

closest match
- USE: relevance ranking

cluster analysis
- UF: clustering
- BT: (research and analytic methods)
- RT: automatic classification

clustering
- USE: cluster analysis

co-occurrence analysis
- UF: cooccurrence analysis
  word co-occurrence analysis
- BT: (research and analytic methods)

co-word analysis
- USE: bibliometrics

coauthors
- BT: authors

coauthorship
- USE: authorship

coaxial cable
- BT: telecommunications equipment

cocitation analysis
- BT: citation analysis
- RT: bibliographic coupling

cognition
- BT: mental processes
- RT: cognitive science
  cognitive styles

cognitive controls
- USE: cognitive styles

cognitive models
- UF: conceptual models
  mental models
- BT: information models
- RT: concepts

cognitive psychology
- USE: cognitive science

cognitive science
- SN: Study of the processes of intelligent reasoning, involving input from disciplines such as psychology, linguistics, and computing science.
- UF: cognitive psychology
- BT: (fields and disciplines)
- RT: cognition
  cognitive styles
  information science

cognitive styles
- SN: Ways in which individuals consistently receive and respond to information.
- UF: cognitive controls
- BT: (human qualities)

cognitive styles (cont.)
- RT: cognition
  cognitive science

collaborative work
- USE: group work

collection assessment
- BT: collection management

collection development
- BT: collection management
  technical services (libraries)
- NT: acquisitions (of materials)
  deselection
  selection (of materials)

collection management
- BT: information resources management
- NT: collection assessment
  collection development
- RT: library materials
  records management

collections
- BT: (by availability, access, organization)
- NT: library collections
  personal collections
  special collections
- RT: core literature

college libraries
- USE: academic libraries

colleges and universities
- UF: academic institutions
  higher education
  universities
- BT: (product and service providers)
- NT: academic libraries
  library schools
- RT: academic freedom

color displays
- BT: displays

COM
- USE: computer output microform

command driven interfaces
- BT: human computer interfaces
- RT: command languages

command languages
    BT: languages
    NT: common command language
    RT: command driven interfaces
          human computer interfaces

common carrier networks
    BT: telecommunications networks

common carriers
    USE: telecommunications industry

common command language
    BT: command languages

common sense knowledge
    UF: world knowledge
    BT: knowledge

communications
    BT: (communications activities)
    NT: authorship
          communications patterns
          communications skills
          disclosure
          electronic communications
          explanation
          face to face communications
          feedback
          informal communications
          negotiation
          oral communications
          organizational communications
          personal networking
          public relations
          publishing
          reading
          storytelling
          telecommunications

communications nctworks
    USE: telecommunications networks

communications patterns
    BT: communications

communications protocols
    UF: network protocols
          protocols
    BT: data transmission
    RT: telecommunications

communications satellites
    USE: satellite communications

communications skills
    BT: communications

communications stars
    USE: gatekeepers

communications theory
    USE: information theory

community based library services
    USE: outreach services (library)

community college libraries
    BT: academic libraries

community information services
    UF: clearinghouses (community
          information)
          I&R services
          information and referral services
          referral services
    BT: information services

community rcsource files
    BT: nonbibliographic databases

compact disc interactive
    UF: CD-I
    BT: compact discs
    RT: CD-ROM

compact disc read only memory
    USE: CD-ROM

compact discs
    UF: CD (compact disks)
          compact disks
    BT: optical discs
    NT: CD-ROM
          compact disc interactive
          digital video interactive

compact disks
    USE: compact discs

compact shelving
    USE: library shelving

compact storage
    BT: storage (materials)

company information
    BT: information
    RT: competitive intelligence

company libraries
    USE: corporate libraries

comparative librarianship
    BT: librarianship

compatibility
  BT: (general qualities)
  RT: connectivity
      data conversion
competition
  BT: (socioeconomic activities)
  RT: competitive intelligence
      private sector
competitive intelligence
  UF: corporate intelligence
  BT: (by content)
  RT: company information
      competition
complexity
  BT: (general qualities)
  RT: reliability
      usability
comprehension
  UF: understanding
  BT: mental processes
compression
  SN: Also use the type of data being
      compressed, e.g., "data," "files,"
      "images."
  UF: data compression
      file compression
  BT: data processing
  RT: signal processing
compulsory deposit
  USE: legal deposit
computational lexicography
  BT: lexicography
computational linguistics
  BT: linguistics
  RT: automatic indexing
computer aided design
  UF: CAD
      interactive design
  BT: (computer operations)
      design
computer aided engineering
  UF: CAE
  BT: (computer operations)
      (technical and manufacturing
      operations)

computer aided instruction
  USE: computer assisted instruction
computer aided manufacturing
  UF: CAM
  BT: (computer operations)
      (technical and manufacturing
      operations)
  RT: computer integrated
      manufacturing
computer aided software engineering
  UF: CASE
      computer assisted software
      engineering
  BT: software engineering
computer aided translation
  USE: machine translation
computer applications
  BT: (computer operations)
computer architectures
  BT: computers
computer assisted instruction
  UF: CAI
      computer aided instruction
  BT: education
computer assisted software engineering
  USE: computer aided software
      engineering
computer centers
  SN: Facilities housing the central
      computer or computers for an
      organization.
  BT: (buildings and facilities)
  RT: computer laboratories
computer conferencing
  BT: computer mediated
      communications
computer crime
  BT: (socioeconomic activities)
  RT: computer security
      data security
      viruses (computer)
computer equipment
  UF: computer hardware
      hardware, computer
  BT: information technology

computer equipment (cont.)
    NT: computer peripherals
            computers
            integrated circuits
computer games
    USE: video games
computer graphics
    BT: graphics
    RT: animation
computer hardware
    USE: computer equipment
computer human interfaces
    USE: human computer interfaces
computer industry
    BT: (product and service providers)
    RT: computers
            software industry
computer integrated manufacturing
    UF: CIM
    BT: (computer operations)
            (technical and manufacturing
            operations)
    RT: computer aided manufacturing
computer laboratories
    SN: Facilities containing multiple
            computers, used for educational
            and class purposes.
    BT: (buildings and facilities)
    RT: computer centers
computer languages
    USE: programming languages
computer learning
    USE: machine learning
computer literacy
    UF: literacy, computer
    BT: (sociocultural aspects)
    RT: information literacy
computer matching
    USE: cross matching
computer mediated communications
    BT: telecommunications
    NT: computer conferencing
            message systems
computer memory
    USE: memory (computer)

computer networks
    USE: telecommunications networks
computer output microfilm
    USE: computer output microform
computer output microform
    UF: COM
            computer output microfilm
    BT: microforms
    RT: microfilm
computer peripherals
    UF: peripherals, computer
    BT: computer equipment
    NT: computer storage
            input equipment
            output equipment
            video display terminals
    RT: computers
computer programming
    UF: programming (computer)
    BT: (computer operations)
    NT: logic programming
            object oriented programming
            software engineering
    RT: computer software
            modularity
            programming languages
computer programs
    USE: computer software
computer resource management
    USE: computing resource management
computer science
    BT: (fields and disciplines)
    NT: dynamic systems
            robotics
    RT: computers
            cybernetics
            information science
computer security
    BT: security
    NT: access control (computer systems)
    RT: computer crime
            data security
computer simulation
    BT: simulation

computer software
- UF: computer programs
  - programs, computer
  - software, computer
- BT: (by medium, physical form)
- NT: artificial intelligence
  - courseware
  - database management systems
  - decision support systems
  - groupware
  - information retrieval systems
  - microprograms
  - operating systems
  - public domain software
  - retrieval software
  - shareware
  - spelling checkers
  - text editors
  - utility software
  - video games
  - virtual reality
  - viruses (computer)
- RT: algorithms
  - computer programming
  - computers
  - programming languages
  - software industry

computer storage
- UF: file systems
  - storage (computer)
- BT: computer peripherals
- NT: archival storage
  - disk drives
  - high density storage

computer systems
- BT: (hardware, equipment, and systems)
- NT: analog systems
  - client server systems
  - dedicated systems
  - human computer interfaces
  - hybrid systems
  - hypercube systems
  - interactive systems
  - turnkey systems

computer systems (cont.)
- RT: computers
  - integrated systems

computer translation
- USE: machine translation

computer typesetting
- USE: typography

computer viruses
- USE: viruses (computer)

computer vision
- UF: machine vision
- BT: artificial intelligence
  - vision
- RT: robotics
  - robots

computerized ...
- USE: automatic...

computerized cataloging
- BT: cataloging (bibliographic)
  - library automation

computers
- BT: computer equipment
- NT: computer architectures
  - database machines
  - file servers
  - mainframe computers
  - memory (computer)
  - microcomputers
  - minicomputers
  - optical computers
  - optoelectronic computers
  - processing units (computers)
  - RISC
  - supercomputers
  - transputers
  - workstations
- RT: computer industry
  - computer peripherals
  - computer science
  - computer software
  - computer systems
  - robots

computing resource management
  UF: computer resource management
       resource management (computing)
  BT: management
concepts
  BT: knowledge
  RT: cognitive models
       index terms
conceptual models
  USE: cognitive models
concordances
  BT: keyword indexes
concurrent processing
  USE: parallel processing
conferences
  USE: meetings
confidential records
  BT: records
  RT: data security
       freedom of information
       medical records
       privacy
       security classification
confidentiality
  USE: privacy
connection tables (chemistry)
  BT: chemical information
       information representations
connectionist models
  BT: models
connectivity
  BT: (qualities of systems and
       equipment)
  RT: compatibility
conservation of library materials
  SN: Physical or chemical strengthening
       of materials.
  BT: preservation of library materials
consistency, interindexer
  USE: indexer consistency
consortia
  BT: organizations
  RT: cooperation
consultants
  UF: consulting services
  BT: (product and service providers)

consulting services
  USE: consultants
consumer information
  BT: information
content addressable memory
  BT: memory (computer)
content analysis
  BT: text processing
contents lists
  UF: table of contents lists
  BT: document surrogates
  RT: SDI services
context free languages
  BT: languages
continuing education
  BT: education
  RT: adult education
       lifelong learning
       workshops
control systems
  BT: (hardware, equipment, and
       systems)
  NT: remote control
controlled vocabularies
  BT: index languages
  NT: subject heading lists
       switching languages
       syndetic structures
       thesauri
       thesaurofacet
  RT: authority files
       classification schemes
       entry vocabularies
       terminology
       vocabulary control
cooccurrence analysis
  USE: co-occurrence analysis
cooperation
  UF: agency cooperation
       interlibrary cooperation
       library cooperation
  BT: (business and management
       operations)
  NT: resource sharing
       shared cataloging

cooperation (cont.)
- RT: consortia
- group work
- interlibrary loans
- library networks
- virtual libraries

cooperative work
- USE: group work

coordinate indexing
- USE: postcoordinate indexing

copiers
- USE: photocopiers

copying
- USE: photocopying

copyright
- BT: intellectual property
- RT: law
- legal aspects
- legal deposit
- public lending right
- royalties
- trade secrets

core literature
- BT: (by information content, purpose)
- RT: Bradford's law
- collections

corporate culture
- USE: organizational culture

corporate intelligence
- USE: competitive intelligence

corporate libraries
- UF: company libraries
- BT: special libraries

corporate name indexing
- USE: name indexing

corporate names
- UF: organization names
- BT: proper names

correction, error
- USE: error correction

correspondence
- UF: letters
- memoranda
- BT: (by information content, purpose)
- RT: records management

correspondence study
- BT: distance learning

cost benefit analysis
- BT: (research and analytic methods)
- RT: decision making

cost effectiveness
- BT: effectiveness

cost recovery
- BT: financial management

costs
- BT: (general qualities)
- NT: overhead costs
- RT: performance

coupling, bibliographic
- USE: bibliographic coupling

courseware
- BT: computer software
- RT: educational technology

CPM
- USE: critical path method

CPU
- USE: processing units (computers)

creativity
- BT: (human qualities)

critical incident method
- BT: management

critical path method
- UF: CPM
- BT: management

cross database searching
- USE: crossfile searching

cross file searching
- USE: crossfile searching

cross matching
- SN: Of data files.
- UF: computer matching
- BT: data processing

cross references
- UF: broader term references
- BT references
- narrower term references
- nonpreferred term references
- NT references
- preferred term references
- related term references
- RT references

cross references (cont.)
    UF: see also references
           see references
           UF references
           use references
           used for references
    BT: syndetic structures
    RT: associative relationships
           equivalence relationships
           hierarchical relationships
           part whole relationships

crossborder data flow
    USE: transborder data flow

crossfile searching
    UF: cross database searching
           cross file searching
           multi database searching
    BT: online searching

CRT terminals
    USE: video display terminals

cryptography
    BT: data processing
    NT: decryption
           encryption

cultural aspects
    USE: social aspects

cumulative indexes
    BT: indexes (information retrieval)

currency (in time)
    UF: timeliness
           up to dateness
    BT: (qualities of information and
           data)
    RT: accuracy
           updating

current awareness services
    BT: information services
    NT: SDI services
    RT: abstracting and indexing services

cybernetics
    BT: (fields and disciplines)
    RT: artificial intelligence
           computer science
           feedback

cybernetics (cont.)
           human computer interfaces
           information science
           stochastic processes

data
    SN: Prefer the specific type of data,
           e.g., "images" or "numeric data."
    BT: (by information content, purpose)
    NT: analog data
           machine readable data
           numeric data
           personal data
    RT: data corruption
           data entry
           databases
           files
           information
           records

data acquisition
    USE: data collection

data analysis
    BT: (research and analytic methods)

data banks
    USE: numeric databases

data capture
    USE: data collection

data collection
    UF: data acquisition
           data capture
    BT: (research and analytic methods)
    RT: data entry
           sensors

data communications
    USE: data transmission

data compression
    USE: compression

data conversion
    UF: document conversion
    BT: data processing
    NT: database conversion
           digital to analog conversion
           digitization
           retrospective conversion
    RT: compatibility

data corruption
    BT: (natural functions and events)
    RT: accuracy
           data
           error detection
           error rates
           errors
           file integrity
           reliability

data dictionaries
    BT: databases

data distribution
    BT: data processing

data entry
    UF: keyboarding
           keying
    BT: data processing
    RT: data
           data collection

data files
    USE: databases

data formats
    UF: formats, data
    BT: (knowledge and information
           organization devices)
    NT: interchange formats

data interchange
    USE: electronic data interchange

data models
    BT: information models
    RT: normalization

data processing
    UF: ADP
           automatic data processing
           DP
           EDP
           electronic data processing
    BT: (computer operations)
    NT: batch processing
           compression
           cross matching
           cryptography
           data conversion
           data distribution
           data entry
           data reduction

data processing (cont.)
    NT: decoding
           encoding
           end user computing
           form filling
           formatting
           multiprocessing
           multitasking
           normalization
           parallel processing
           pattern recognition
           real time processing
           scanning
           sorting
           validation
           verification
           word processing
    RT: information production

data processors
    USE: processing units (computers)

data protection
    USE: data security

data reduction
    SN: The transformation of a set of
           raw data into a more useful form.
    BT: data processing

data representation
    USE: knowledge representation

data security
    UF: data protection
    BT: security
    RT: computer crime
           computer security
           confidential records
           information policy
           personal data
           privacy

data sets
    USE: numeric databases

data structures
    BT: (knowledge and information
           organization devices)
    NT: abstract data types
           tree structures
    RT: databases

data transmission
UF: data communications
BT: telecommunications
NT: broadband transmission
communications protocols
digital communications
electronic data interchange
electronic filing
file transfers
voice transmission

databanks
USE: numeric databases

database conversion
BT: data conversion

database design
BT: design
organization of information

database hosts
USE: search services

database indexing
BT: indexing
RT: periodical indexing

database leasing
UF: leasing, database
tape leasing
BT: (information and library
operations)
RT: database producers
financial management
search services

database machines
BT: computers
RT: databases

database maintenance
BT: maintenance
RT: databases

database management systems
UF: file systems
BT: computer software
RT: databases

database models
BT: models
NT: relational models
RT: databases

database producers
BT: publishers
NT: abstracting and indexing services
RT: database leasing
information industry
information infrastructure
online industry
search services

database vendors
USE: search services

databases
UF: data files
BT: (by information content, purpose)
NT: bibliographic databases
data dictionaries
deductive databases
distributed databases
nonbibliographic databases
object oriented databases
online databases
relational databases
RT: abstracting and indexing services
abstracts
data
data structures
database machines
database maintenance
database management systems
database models
files
indexes (information retrieval)
knowledge bases
periodical indexes
value added

DDC
USE: Dewey Decimal Classification

deaf persons
USE: disabled persons

decentralization
BT: (business and management
operations)
RT: centralization

decision making
- BT: (research and analytic methods)
- RT: cost benefit analysis
  decision support systems
  decision theory

decision support systems
- UF: DSS
- BT: computer software
- NT: group decision support systems
- RT: decision making
  executive information systems
  management
  management information systems

decision theory
- BT: (fields and disciplines)
- RT: decision making

decoding
- BT: data processing
- RT: decryption

decryption
- BT: cryptography
- RT: decoding

dedicated systems
- BT: computer systems

deductive databases
- SN: Databases in which new facts can be derived from facts currently in the database by application of rules.
- BT: databases
- RT: expert systems

default values
- BT: (by content)

definitions (of terms)
- USE: terminology

delivery of documents
- USE: document delivery

demographics
- BT: social sciences

depository libraries
- BT: libraries
- RT: government publications

depth (indexing)
- UF: indexing depth
- BT: (qualities of information and data)

depth (indexing) (cont.)
- RT: exhaustivity (indexing)
  indexing
  specificity (indexing)

derivative indexing
- UF: free text indexing
- BT: indexing

descriptive bibliography
- USE: analytical bibliography

descriptive cataloging
- UF: bibliographic description
- BT: cataloging (bibliographic)

descriptors
- SN: Terms of a controlled vocabulary, authorized for use in indexing.
- BT: index terms
- RT: subject headings
  thesauri

deselection
- UF: weeding
- BT: collection development

design
- BT: (general activities)
- NT: computer aided design
  database design
  forms design
  screen design

desktop computers
- USE: personal computers

desktop metaphor
- BT: metaphors
- RT: graphical user interfaces

desktop publishing
- BT: publishing
- RT: WYSIWYG

detection, error
- USE: error detection

Dewey Decimal Classification
- UF: DDC
- BT: classification schemes

diacriticals
- SN: Signs used to indicate different values, semantic or phonetic, of alphabetic characters.
- BT: information representations
- RT: character sets

dictionaries
 UF: glossaries
 BT: reference materials
 RT: encyclopedias
  terminology
  thesauri

diffusion of innovation
 BT: (socioeconomic activities)
 RT: innovation
  technology transfer

digests
 SN: Condensed versions of
  documents; for digests of
  periodical articles use "abstracts."
 UF: summaries
 BT: document surrogates
 RT: abstracts

digital audio tapes
 BT: audiotapes

digital communications
 BT: data transmission
 RT: digital to analog conversion
  digitization

digital to analog conversion
 BT: data conversion
 RT: digital communications

digital video interactive
 UF: DV-I
 BT: compact discs
 RT: CD-ROM

digitization
 UF: analog to digital conversion
 BT: data conversion
 RT: digital communications
  digitized images

digitized images
 BT: images
 RT: digitization

direct read after write technology
 USE: DRAW

directories
 BT: reference materials

disabled persons
 UF: blind persons
  deaf persons

disabled persons (cont.)
 UF: handicapped persons
  physically challenged persons
 BT: (persons and informal groups)
 NT: learning disabled persons
  reading disabled persons

disambiguation
 BT: linguistic analysis
 RT: ambiguity
  homography

disasters
 BT: (natural functions and events)

disclosure
 BT: communications
 RT: ethics
  freedom of information
  privacy

discourse analysis
 SN: Processing of multi-sentence texts.
 BT: natural language processing

discourse generation
 SN: Generation of multi-sentence
  texts.
 BT: natural language processing

discs
 USE: disks

disk drives
 BT: computer storage
 NT: CD-ROM drives
 RT: disks

disks
 UF: discs
 BT: (physical media)
 NT: magnetic disks
  optical discs
 RT: disk drives

displays
 SN: Video displays.
 BT: (hardware, equipment, and
  systems)
 NT: color displays
  high resolution displays
  video display terminals

displays (thesauri)
 USE: thesaurus displays

dissertations
UF: theses
BT: (by information content, purpose)
distance education
USE: distance learning
distance learning
UF: distance education
BT: education
NT: correspondence study
RT: lifelong learning
      off campus education
distributed computing
BT: (computer operations)
RT: distributed databases
distributed databases
BT: databases
RT: distributed computing
document access
BT: access to resources
RT: bibliographic access
document conversion
USE: data conversion
document delivery
UF: delivery of documents
BT: (information and library
      operations)
NT: facsimile transmission
      interlibrary loans
RT: document retrieval
      virtual libraries
document handling
BT: (information and library
      operations)
document representations
USE: document surrogates
document retrieval
BT: (information and library
      operations)
RT: document delivery
      information retrieval
document storage
USE: storage (materials)
document surrogates
UF: document representations
      representations, document
      surrogates, document

document surrogates (cont.)
BT: (by information content, purpose)
NT: abstracts
      annotations
      bibliographic records
      contents lists
      digests
      standard book numbers
      standard serial numbers
document use
USE: information use
documentary languages
BT: index languages
documentation
SN: Of software, hardware, and
      systems. For the theoretical
      meaning, use "information
      science."
BT: (computer operations)
      (information and library
      operations)
RT: help systems
      user aids
domain knowledge
BT: knowledge
RT: task knowledge
downloading
BT: file transfers
RT: online searching
DP
USE: data processing
DRAM
UF: dynamic RAM
      dynamic random access memory
BT: random access memory
DRAW
UF: direct read after write technology
BT: WORM discs
drawings, engineering
USE: engineering drawings
drugs
USE: pharmacology
DSS
USE: decision support systems

duplicate detection
    BT: quality control
    RT: duplicate records
           error detection

duplicate records
    BT: records
    RT: duplicate detection

durability
    BT: (general qualities)
    RT: maintainability
           performance
           permanence
           reliability

DV-I
    USE: digital video interactive

dynamic RAM
    USE: DRAM

dynamic random access memory
    USE: DRAM

dynamic systems
    BT: computer science

dyslexia
    USE: reading disabled persons

e-mail
    USE: electronic mail

early adopters
    BT: (persons and informal groups)
    RT: innovation

earth sciences
    BT: natural sciences

ease of use
    USE: usability

ecology
    BT: natural sciences

econometrics
    BT: economics
           measurement

economic indicators
    USE: indicators (values)

economics
    BT: social sciences
    NT: econometrics
           economics of information

economics of information
    UF: information economics
           value of information

economics of information (cont.)
    BT: economics
           information science
    RT: information society

EDI
    USE: electronic data interchange

editing
    BT: text processing
    RT: editors
           markup languages
           proofreading

editors
    SN: Persons; for software use "text
           editors."
    BT: information professionals
    RT: editing

EDP
    USE: data processing

education
    UF: instruction
           teaching
    BT: social sciences
    NT: adult education
           basic education
           computer assisted instruction
           continuing education
           distance learning
           home education
           information science education
           library education
           off campus education
    RT: accreditation
           educational technology
           reading
           students
           training

educational technology
    SN: Limit to general information. For
           specific technologies, use the
           name of the technology, e.g.
           computer networks.
    UF: instructional technology
    BT: (hardware, equipment, and
           systems)
    RT: courseware
           education

effectiveness
    BT: (general qualities)
    NT: cost effectiveness
          retrieval effectiveness
    RT: evaluation
          indexer consistency
          performance
          usability
efficiency
    BT: (general qualities)
EFTS
    USE: electronic funds transfer systems
EIS
    USE: executive information systems
electronic bulletin boards
    USE: bulletin board systems
electronic communications
    BT: communications
    NT: error messages
electronic data interchange
    UF: data interchange
          EDI
    BT: data transmission
    RT: electronic funds transfer systems
          interchange formats
electronic data processing
    USE: data processing
electronic document interchange formats
    USE: interchange formats
electronic filing
    SN: Submission of in electronic form
          rather than on paper, especially
          of required government forms.
    BT: data transmission
electronic funds transfer systems
    UF: EFTS
    BT: (computer operations)
    RT: electronic data interchange
electronic imaging
    USE: imaging
electronic information products
    USE: electronic publications
electronic information systems
    USE: information retrieval systems

electronic journals
    BT: electronic publications
          journals
electronic libraries
    USE: library automation
electronic mail
    UF: e-mail
          email
    BT: message systems
electronic offices
    USE: office automation
electronic publications
    UF: electronic information products
    BT: (by medium, physical form)
          publications
    NT: electronic journals
    RT: electronic publishing
electronic publishing
    BT: publishing
    RT: electronic publications
email
    USE: electronic mail
empirical studies
    BT: research and development
employees
    UF: personnel
    BT: (persons and informal groups)
employment
    BT: (socioeconomic activities)
    NT: working at home
    RT: information workers
encoding
    BT: data processing
    NT: hash coding
          superimposed coding
    RT: encryption
encryption
    SN: Modification of stored data using
          a transformation algorithm, in
          order to render the data
          incomprehensible to unauthorized
          examiners.
    BT: cryptography
    RT: encoding

encyclopedias
BT: reference materials
RT: dictionaries

end user computing
BT: data processing
RT: end users

end user searching
BT: searching
RT: end users

end users
BT: users
NT: novice users
RT: end user computing
end user searching
information society

engineering
BT: (fields and disciplines)

engineering drawings
UF: drawings, engineering
BT: (by medium, physical form)

English language
BT: languages

entrepreneurs
BT: (persons and informal groups)
RT: entrepreneurship

entrepreneurship
BT: (socioeconomic activities)
RT: entrepreneurs
innovation

entries
SN: Records of items in files; normally used with regard to library catalogs and indexes.
UF: catalog entries
index entries
BT: access points
RT: authority files

entropy (information)
BT: (natural functions and events)
RT: information theory

entry vocabularies
SN: The nonpreferred terms in a controlled vocabulary, leading to the preferred terms which are used in indexing.
UF: access vocabularies

entry vocabularies (cont.)
BT: access points
RT: controlled vocabularies

ephemera
BT: (by information content, purpose)

equivalence relationships
UF: synonymous relationships
synonymy
UF relationships
use relationships
used for relationships
BT: semantic relationships
NT: quasi-synonymous relationships
RT: cross references

erasable optical discs
UF: rewritable optical disks
BT: optical discs

ergonomics
BT: human factors

erotic materials
BT: (by information content, purpose)
RT: pornographic materials

error correction
UF: correction, error
BT: quality control
RT: accuracy
error detection
error rates
errors
evaluation
fault tolerance
reliability
validation
verification

error detection
UF: detection, error
BT: quality control
RT: accuracy
data corruption
duplicate detection
error correction
error messages
error rates
errors
evaluation
fault tolerance

error detection (cont.)
   RT: reliability
         validation
         verification

error messages
   BT: electronic communications
         human computer interfaces
   RT: error detection
         errors
         help systems
         validation

error rates
   BT: (qualities of information and data)
   RT: accuracy
         data corruption
         error correction
         error detection
         errors
         evaluation
         reliability
         validation
         verification

errors
   BT: (by content)
   NT: typographical errors
   RT: accuracy
         data corruption
         error correction
         error detection
         error messages
         error rates
         evaluation
         fault tolerance
         reliability
         validation
         verification

ethics
   BT: (sociocultural aspects)
   RT: disclosure

etymology
   BT: linguistics
   RT: words

evaluation
   BT: (general activities)

evaluation (cont.)
   NT: benchmarks
         refereeing
         reviewing
   RT: accreditation
         effectiveness
         error correction
         error detection
         error rates
         errors
         indexer consistency
         monitoring
         noise (information retrieval)
         quality
         quality control
         recall
         relevance
         relevance judgments
         research and development
         retrieval effectiveness
         standardization

exact match searching
   BT: searching

exchange formats
   USE: interchange formats

exchanges (of materials)
   USE: gifts and exchanges

executive information systems
   UF: EIS
   BT: information retrieval systems
   RT: decision support systems
         management information systems

exhaustivity (indexing)
   UF: indexing exhaustivity
   BT: (qualities of information and data)
   RT: depth (indexing)
         indexing
         specificity (indexing)

experiments
   BT: (research and analytic methods)
   RT: testing

expert systems
   UF: knowledge based systems
   BT: artificial intelligence

expert systems (cont.)
    RT: deductive databases
             knowledge acquisition
             knowledge bases
             knowledge engineering
experts, subject
    USE: subject experts
explanation
    BT: communications
extension campuses
    USE: off campus education
extracting
    UF: extraction
    BT: summarization
    NT: automatic extracting
extraction
    USE: extracting
face to face communications
    BT: communications
    NT: meetings
             nonverbal communications
    RT: meetings
             oral communications
facet analysis
    BT: organization of information
    RT: faceted classification
             index language construction
             indexing
facet formula
    USE: citation order
faceted classification
    BT: classification
    RT: citation order
             facet analysis
             thesaurofacet
facsimile transmission
    UF: fax
             telefacsimile
    BT: document delivery
             telecommunications
    RT: image processing
fact databases
    UF: factual databases
    BT: nonbibliographic databases
    NT: numeric databases
    RT: fact retrieval systems

fact retrieval systems
    UF: question answering systems
    BT: information retrieval systems
    RT: answer passage retrieval
             fact databases
factor analysis
    BT: mathematical methods
    RT: statistical methods
factual databases
    USE: fact databases
fallout
    SN: A measure of retrieval
             effectiveness; the ratio of
             nonrelevant items retrieved by a
             query to the total number of
             nonrelevant items in the database.
    BT: (qualities of information and
             data)
    RT: noise (information retrieval)
             precision
             recall
             relevance
             retrieval effectiveness
false drops
    USE: noise (information retrieval)
fault tolerance
    BT: (qualities of systems and
             equipment)
    RT: error correction
             error detection
             errors
             reliability
fax
    USE: facsimile transmission
feature extraction
    BT: optical character recognition
    RT: font learning
feedback
    SN: Communications; not electronic
             feedback.
    UF: user feedback
    BT: communications
    RT: cybernetics
             similarity
fees
    USE: pricing

fees for service
    BT: pricing

fiber optics
    UF: optical fibers
    BT: telecommunications equipment

fiction
    UF: novels
    BT: literature
    RT: books

file compression
    USE: compression

file integrity
    BT: (qualities of information and data)
    RT: data corruption
          files
          reliability

file servers
    UF: network servers
    BT: computers
    NT: image servers
    RT: client server systems
          local area networks

file structures
    BT: (knowledge and information organization devices)
    NT: hierarchical file structures

file systems
    USE: database management systems

file systems
    USE: information retrieval systems

file systems
    USE: computer storage

file transfers
    BT: data transmission
    NT: downloading
          uploading
    RT: files

files
    SN: Collections of records, each collection involving a set of entities with certain aspects in common and organized for a specific purpose.
    UF: machine readable files
    BT: (by information content, purpose)

files (cont.)
    NT: authority files
          inverted files
          personal files
    RT: data
          databases
          file integrity
          file transfers

filing
    USE: arrangement

films
    SN: Use for information recorded in film form; for the physical material use "photographic films."
    UF: motion pictures
    BT: visual materials
    RT: records
          visual materials

filmstrips
    BT: visual materials
    RT: visual materials

filtering, information
    USE: information filtering

finance
    BT: (fields and disciplines)
    RT: financial management

financial management
    UF: funding
    BT: management
    NT: budgeting
          cost recovery
          grants
    RT: accounting
          database leasing
          finance

fine arts
    BT: (fields and disciplines)
    NT: art
          music
    RT: architecture

finite element analysis
    BT: mathematical methods

flexible disks
    USE: floppy disks

flexible manufacturing systems
BT: (technical and manufacturing operations)

floppy disks
UF: flexible disks
BT: magnetic disks

floptical discs
BT: optical discs
RT: optical equipment

flow charting
BT: (computer operations)
RT: systems analysis
systems design

focus groups
BT: (persons and informal groups)
RT: marketing
user studies

font learning
BT: machine learning
optical character recognition
RT: feature extraction

forecasting
UF: future
prediction
BT: (research and analytic methods)
RT: planning
strategic planning

foreign language materials
SN: Use for information about foreign language materials, not for materials in a foreign language.
BT: (by availability, access, organization)
RT: foreign languages
multilingual thesauri

foreign languages
SN: Languages other than English.
BT: languages
RT: foreign language materials
language barriers
multilingual subject indexing
multilingual thesauri

forenames
USE: personal names

form filling
BT: data processing

formats, data
USE: data formats

formatting
BT: data processing

forms design
BT: design

Fourier analysis
UF: Fourier transforms
BT: mathematical methods

Fourier transforms
USE: Fourier analysis

frame based systems
USE: knowledge bases

free text indexing
USE: keywords

free text indexing
USE: derivative indexing

free text searching
SN: Searching of text of full documents or parts of documents.
BT: searching
NT: full text searching

freedom of information
BT: intellectual freedom
RT: censorship
confidential records
disclosure
public records

freedom to read
BT: intellectual freedom
RT: banned materials
censorship

frequency of use
UF: term frequency
usage frequency
BT: (qualities of information and data)
NT: word frequency
RT: information use

friends of libraries
UF: friends of the library organizations
BT: organizations

friends of the library organizations
USE: friends of libraries

front ends
- BT: human computer interfaces
- RT: gateways

fugitive materials
- USE: alternative publications

full motion video
- USE: motion video

full text databases
- UF: full text information systems
  full text systems
  text databases
  textbases
  textual databases
- BT: bibliographic databases
- RT: full text searching
  keywords

full text information systems
- USE: full text databases

full text retrieval
- USE: full text searching

full text searching
- SN: Searching of text of full documents.
- UF: full text retrieval
  text retrieval
- BT: free text searching
- RT: full text databases
  keyword searching
  natural language processing
  online searching

full text systems
- USE: full text databases

functional literacy
- USE: literacy

funding
- USE: financial management

future
- USE: forecasting

fuzzy logic
- USE: fuzzy set theory

fuzzy retrieval systems
- UF: fuzzy search
  partial match retrieval systems
- BT: information retrieval systems
- RT: relevance ranking
  searching

fuzzy search
- USE: fuzzy retrieval systems

fuzzy set theory
- UF: fuzzy logic
- BT: set theory
- RT: set theory

game theory
- BT: mathematical methods
- RT: mathematics

gatekeepers
- UF: bridge agents
  communications stars
  liaison agents
  technological gatekeepers
- BT: (persons and informal groups)
- RT: human information sources
  information filtering
  information flow
  personal networking

gateway services
- USE: gateways

gateways
- UF: gateway services
- BT: human computer interfaces
- RT: front ends

gender
- BT: (sociocultural aspects)

genealogy
- BT: (information and library operations)
- RT: archives

generalization
- BT: mental processes
- RT: abstraction

generic posting
- SN: Posting of items under both specific and more general headings.
- BT: subject indexing

generic relationships
- USE: genus species relationships

genomes
- BT: (by content)
- RT: biomedical sciences

genus species relationships
UF: generic relationships
BT: hierarchical relationships
geographic information systems
UF: GIS
BT: information retrieval systems
geographic location
USE: physical location
geography
BT: natural sciences
gifts and exchanges
UF: exchanges (of materials)
BT: acquisitions (of materials)
GIS
USE: geographic information systems
global village
USE: information society
glossaries
USE: dictionaries
goals
UF: objectives
BT: (sociocultural aspects)
RT: planning
government agencies
BT: (product and service providers)
NT: state library agencies
RT: public sector
government documents
USE: government publications
government libraries
BT: libraries
NT: state libraries
government policy
USE: public policy
government publications
UF: government documents
BT: publications
RT: depository libraries
         technical reports
grammars
BT: linguistics
NT: case grammar
grants
BT: financial management
graph processing
BT: information processing

graph theory
BT: mathematical methods
RT: mathematics
graphic images
USE: graphics
graphical representations
USE: icons
graphical thesauri
BT: thesauri
graphical user interfaces
UF: GUI
         windows interfaces
BT: human computer interfaces
RT: desktop metaphor
         icons
         mice (computer peripherals)
         trackballs (computer peripherals)
         WYSIWYG
graphics
UF: graphic images
BT: (by medium, physical form)
NT: computer graphics
         sociograms
RT: illustrations
         images
         WYSIWYG
graphics terminals
USE: video display terminals
graphs
BT: information representations
grey literature
UF: near-published literature
BT: (by availability, access,
         organization)
NT: preprints
         technical reports
RT: alternative publications
         technical reports
group decision support systems
BT: decision support systems
RT: group work
         groupware
group work
UF: collaborative work
         cooperative work

group work (cont.)
- BT: (business and management operations)
- RT: cooperation
  group decision support systems
  groupware

groupware
- SN: Computer software designed to support collaborative work.
- BT: computer software
- RT: group decision support systems
  group work

growth
- BT: (natural functions and events)
- RT: bibliometrics
  change

GUI
- USE: graphical user interfaces

guidelines
- USE: standards

half life of literatures
- USE: aging of literatures

handbooks
- BT: reference materials

handicapped persons
- USE: disabled persons

handwritten input
- USE: pen based computing

hard disks
- BT: magnetic disks

hardware, computer
- USE: computer equipment

hash coding
- UF: hashing
- BT: encoding

hashing
- USE: hash coding

HDTV
- UF: high definition television
- BT: television
- RT: high resolution displays

headings
- SN: Terms under which entries are made in indexes or catalogues; usually used in the print context.

headings (cont.)
- BT: access points
- RT: index terms

health sciences
- USE: biomedical sciences

hedges (online searching)
- BT: search strategies

help systems
- BT: human computer interfaces
- RT: documentation
  error messages
  user aids

heuristics
- SN: Methods of problem solving in which increases in efficiency may be traded off against finding a good solution which may not be the best possible solution.
- BT: problem solving

hierarchical classification
- BT: classification

hierarchical file structures
- BT: file structures

hierarchical models
- BT: models

hierarchical relationships
- UF: broader term relationships
  BT relationships
  narrower term relationships
  NT relationships
- BT: semantic relationships
- NT: genus species relationships
  part whole relationships
- RT: cross references
  part whole relationships

hierarchies
- BT: (knowledge and information organization devices)

high definition television
- USE: HDTV

high density storage
- BT: computer storage

high level languages
- BT: programming languages

high performance computing
- USE: supercomputers

high resolution displays
    BT: displays
    RT: HDTV
higher education
    USE: colleges and universities
historical bibliography
    USE: analytical bibliography
historical records
    USE: archives
history
    BT: humanities
holdings (library)
    USE: library collections
holographic memory
    BT: memory (computer)
    RT: holography
holography
    BT: (computer operations)
    RT: holographic memory
home education
    BT: education
home information services
    BT: information services
home work
    USE: working at home
homography
    BT: semantic relationships
    RT: disambiguation
host computers
    USE: client server systems
host computers
    USE: bibliographic utilities
host computers
    USE: search services
host services
    USE: search services
Hough transformation
    BT: mathematical methods
human behavior
    UF: behavior, human
    BT: (sociocultural aspects)
    NT: user behavior
    RT: attitudes
           psychological aspects
           psychology

human computer interaction
    USE: human computer interfaces
human computer interfaces
    UF: computer human interfaces
           human computer interaction
           interfaces
           man machine interfaces
           user system interfaces
    BT: computer systems
    NT: audio interfaces
           command driven interfaces
           error messages
           front ends
           gateways
           graphical user interfaces
           help systems
           intelligent interfaces
           menu based interfaces
           touch screen interfaces
    RT: command languages
           cybernetics
           look and feel
           navigation
           screen design
human engineering
    USE: human factors
human factors
    UF: human engineering
    BT: (fields and disciplines)
    NT: ergonomics
human indexing
    USE: manual indexing
human information sources
    BT: (persons and informal groups)
           information sources
    RT: gatekeepers
           personal networking
human resource files
    BT: nonbibliographic databases
human resource management
    BT: management
    RT: information workers

humanities
BT: (fields and disciplines)
NT: history
       lexicography
       linguistics
       literature
       logic
       philosophy
hybrid systems
BT: computer systems
hypercube systems
BT: computer systems
hyperdocuments
USE: hypertext
hypermedia
BT: (by medium, physical form)
RT: authoring (hypermedia)
       hypertext
       nonprint media
hypertext
UF: hyperdocuments
BT: (by medium, physical form)
RT: authoring (hypermedia)
       hypermedia
       links (hypertext)
hypertext links
USE: links (hypertext)
I&R services
USE: community information services
IAC
USE: information analysis centers
iconography
USE: images
icons
SN: Graphical interface objects.
UF: graphical representations
BT: information representations
RT: graphical user interfaces
identification
BT: (general activities)
identifiers
SN: Uncontrolled terms used in
       indexing, usually terms such as
       proper names or jargon which are
       not eligible to become descriptors.

identifiers (cont.)
BT: index terms
RT: name indexing
ideographs
BT: writing systems
idioms
BT: information representations
RT: languages
ILL
USE: interlibrary loans
illiteracy
USE: literacy
illustrations
BT: (by medium, physical form)
RT: graphics
       image information systems
       images
image analysis
BT: image processing
RT: image enhancement
       images
image data
USE: images
image databases
BT: nonbibliographic databases
RT: images
image enhancement
BT: image processing
RT: image analysis
image information
USE: images
image information systems
UF: pictorial information systems
BT: information retrieval systems
RT: art
       illustrations
       image retrieval
       images
image processing
BT: information processing
NT: image analysis
       image enhancement
RT: facsimile transmission
       images
       imaging
       signal processing

image retrieval
- BT: information retrieval
- RT: image information systems
  - images

image servers
- BT: file servers

images
- UF: iconography
  - image data
  - image information
- BT: visual materials
- NT: bit-mapped images
  - digitized images
  - photographs
- RT: art
  - graphics
  - illustrations
  - image analysis
  - image databases
  - image information systems
  - image processing
  - image retrieval
  - imaging

imaging
- UF: electronic imaging
- BT: (computer operations)
- NT: magnetic resonance imaging
  - tomography
- RT: image processing
  - images

indecent materials
- USE: pornographic materials

index entries
- USE: entries

index language construction
- UF: classification construction
  - taxonomy construction
  - thesaurus construction
- BT: organization of information
- RT: classification schemes
  - facet analysis
  - index languages
  - literary warrant
  - thesauri
  - thesaurus maintenance
  - vocabulary control

index languages
- UF: indexing languages
  - links (hypermedia)
  - retrieval languages
  - search languages
- BT: languages
- NT: classification schemes
  - controlled vocabularies
  - documentary languages
- RT: index language construction
  - index terms
  - indexes (information retrieval)
  - indexing
  - information retrieval
  - links (between indexing terms)
  - role indicators
  - subject indexing

index term weighting
- USE: weighting

index terms
- SN: Terms used in indexing.
- UF: indexing terms
  - subject index terms
  - used terms
- BT: terms
- NT: candidate descriptors
  - descriptors
  - identifiers
  - keywords
  - modifiers
  - qualifiers
  - subject headings
  - top terms
- RT: citation order
  - classification
  - concepts
  - headings
  - index languages
  - indexing
  - search terms
  - thesauri
  - weighting

indexer consistency
- SN: The extent to which different indexers, or the same indexer at different times, assign the same index terms to a given document.
- UF: consistency, interindexer
- BT: (human qualities)
- RT: effectiveness
  evaluation
  indexing
  reliability
  testing

indexes (information retrieval)
- BT: (by information content, purpose)
- NT: alphabetico classed indexes
  author indexes
  author-prepared indexes
  book indexes
  citation indexes
  cumulative indexes
  keyword indexes
  periodical indexes
  subject indexes
- RT: abstracting and indexing services
  bibliographic databases
  bibliographies
  catalogs (bibliographic)
  databases
  index languages
  indexing

indexing
- BT: organization of information
- NT: assignment indexing
  automatic indexing
  book indexing
  database indexing
  derivative indexing
  manual indexing
  name indexing
  periodical indexing
  probabilistic indexing
  string indexing
  subject indexing

indexing (cont.)
- RT: aboutness
  abstracting and indexing services
  authority files
  classification
  classification schemes
  depth (indexing)
  exhaustivity (indexing)
  facet analysis
  index languages
  index terms
  indexer consistency
  indexes (information retrieval)
  literary warrant
  specificity (indexing)
  weighting

indexing depth
- USE: depth (indexing)

indexing exhaustivity
- USE: exhaustivity (indexing)

indexing languages
- USE: index languages

indexing services
- USE: abstracting and indexing services

indexing terms
- USE: index terms

indicators (values)
- UF: economic indicators
- BT: (by content)

individual differences
- BT: (sociocultural aspects)

industry
- USE: business

inference
- BT: reasoning

infometrics
- UF: cliometrics
  informetrics
- BT: measurement
- NT: bibliometrics
  scientometrics
  Zipf's law

informal communications
- BT: communications
- RT: oral communications
  organizational communications

informatics
    USE: information technology
informatics
    SN: An emerging area of activity
            which represents the conjunction
            of information science and
            information technology.
    BT: (fields and disciplines)
    NT: medical informatics
            museum informatics
    RT: information science
            information technology
informatics, medical
    USE: medical informatics
informatics, museum
    USE: museum informatics
information
    SN: Very broad term; prefer specific
            type or aspect, e.g., "consumer
            information" or "information
            access." Or also use the subject,
            e.g., "finance."
    BT: (by content)
    NT: company information
            consumer information
            public information
            scientific and technical
            information
    RT: data
            knowledge
information access
    UF: availability of information
    BT: access to resources
    NT: subject access
    RT: bibliographic access
            library access
information analysis centers
    UF: clearinghouses (information
            analysis)
            IAC
            information centers (information
            analysis)
    BT: (product and service providers)
    RT: information industry
information and referral services
    USE: community information services

information associations
    BT: professional associations
information brokers
    BT: (product and service providers)
    RT: information industry
            information professionals
            online searchers
information centers (information analysis)
    USE: information analysis centers
information centers (libraries)
    USE: libraries
information centers (special libraries)
    USE: special libraries
information dissemination
    BT: (information and library
            operations)
    RT: information resources
            management
            SDI services
information economics
    USE: economics of information
information engineering
    USE: knowledge engineering
information exchange
    USE: information transfer
information exchange formats
    USE: interchange formats
information explosion
    UF: publication explosion
    BT: (natural functions and events)
    RT: information overload
            publishing
information filtering
    UF: filtering, information
    BT: information flow
    RT: gatekeepers
            personal networking
information flow
    BT: (information and library
            operations)
    NT: information filtering
            transborder data flow
    RT: gatekeepers
            information resources
            management
            personal networking

information industry
- BT: (product and service providers)
- NT: online industry
- RT: database producers
  information analysis centers
  information brokers
  information infrastructure
  information utilities
  publishers
  search services
  telecommunications industry

information infrastructure
- BT: (product and service providers)
- RT: abstracting and indexing services
  database producers
  information industry
  information utilities
  libraries
  publishers
  search services

information life cycle
- BT: (natural functions and events)
- RT: aging of materials
  obsolescence

information literacy
- UF: information skills
  literacy, information
- BT: (sociocultural aspects)
- RT: bibliographic instruction
  computer literacy
  information needs
  information use
  literacy
  user training

information management
- USE: information resources
  management

information models
- BT: models
- NT: cognitive models
  data models

information needs
- UF: user information needs
  user needs
- BT: (human qualities)

information needs (cont.)
- RT: information literacy
  information resources
  management
  information seeking
  information use
  needs assessment
  users

information networks
- USE: telecommunications networks

information overload
- UF: overload, information
- BT: (sociocultural aspects)
- RT: information explosion
  information society
  information use

information policy
- BT: public policy
- RT: data security
  information society
  legal aspects
  politics
  privacy

information processing
- BT: (computer operations)
- NT: graph processing
  image processing
  query processing
  romanization
  text processing
  translation
  transliteration
  truncation
  weighting
- RT: automatic indexing
  information science
  knowledge representation

information production
- BT: (information and library operations)
- RT: data processing
  publishing

information products
- USE: publications

information professionals
UF: information professions
information specialists
professionals
BT: information workers
NT: archivists
editors
information scientists
librarians
media specialists
online searchers
records managers
translators
RT: information brokers
information professions
USE: information professionals
information representations
BT: (information representations)
NT: abbreviations
acronyms
anaphora
bar codes
character sets
chemical structures
connection tables (chemistry)
diacriticals
graphs
icons
idioms
metaphors
notation
symbols
terminology
terms
writing systems
RT: information science
information resources management
UF: information management
IRM
resource management
(information)
BT: (information and library
operations)
management
NT: collection management
records management

information resources management (cont.)
RT: information dissemination
information flow
information needs
library management
records management
information retrieval
BT: (information and library
operations)
NT: answer passage retrieval
associative retrieval
image retrieval
probabilistic retrieval
searching
RT: document retrieval
index languages
information retrieval systems
information science
natural language processing
relevance judgments
retrieval effectiveness
retrieval software
information retrieval systems
UF: electronic information systems
file systems
information storage and retrieval
systems
information systems
online information retrieval
systems
online systems
search systems
BT: computer software
NT: executive information systems
fact retrieval systems
fuzzy retrieval systems
geographic information systems
image information systems
management information systems
paper based information systems
reference retrieval systems
RT: aboutness
information retrieval
online searching
relevance

information science
- BT: (fields and disciplines)
- NT: economics of information
  - information theory
- RT: cognitive science
  - computer science
  - cybernetics
  - informatics
  - information processing
  - information representations
  - information retrieval
  - information science education
  - information scientists
  - librarianship
  - linguistics

information science education
- BT: education
- RT: information science
  - library education

information scientists
- BT: information professionals
- RT: information science

information sector (economy)
- BT: (sectors of the economy)

information seeking
- BT: (information and library operations)
- RT: information needs
  - information use
  - personal networking

information services
- SN: For information service publishers, use "database producers" or "abstracting and indexing services."
- BT: (information and library operations)
- NT: community information services
  - current awareness services
  - home information services
  - litigation support
- RT: library services
  - value added

information skills
- USE: information literacy

information society
- SN: The concept of society in which information is the driving force of the economy, with global availability of communication and large-scale production of information.
- UF: global village
- BT: (sociocultural aspects)
- RT: economics of information
  - end users
  - information overload
  - information policy

information sources
- BT: (by information content, purpose)
- NT: human information sources

information specialists
- USE: information professionals

information storage and retrieval systems
- USE: information retrieval systems

information systems
- USE: information retrieval systems

information technology
- UF: informatics
- BT: (hardware, equipment, and systems)
- NT: computer equipment
- RT: informatics
  - library equipment
  - telecommunications

information theory
- UF: communications theory
- BT: information science
- RT: entropy (information)

information transfer
- UF: information exchange
- BT: (information and library operations)

information use
- UF: document use
  - information utilization
  - library use
  - use of information
- BT: (information and library operations)

information use (cont.)
  RT: bibliometrics
       frequency of use
       information literacy
       information needs
       information overload
       information seeking
       library users
       users
information user studies
  USE: user studies
information users
  USE: users
information utilities
  BT: (product and service providers)
  RT: bibliographic utilities
       information industry
       information infrastructure
       online industry
       search services
information utilization
  USE: information use
information workers
  UF: knowledge workers
  BT: (persons and informal groups)
  NT: information professionals
       library personnel
  RT: employment
       human resource management
informetrics
  USE: infometrics
initialisms
  USE: acronyms
innovation
  UF: technological innovation
  BT: (socioeconomic activities)
  RT: diffusion of innovation
       early adopters
       entrepreneurship
       patents
       technology impact
input equipment
  BT: computer peripherals
  NT: joysticks
       keyboards
       light pens

input equipment (cont.)
  NT: pointing devices
       scanners
  RT: sensors
       video display terminals
institutional libraries
  BT: libraries
instruction
  USE: education
instructional technology
  USE: educational technology
instrumentation
  BT: (hardware, equipment, and
       systems)
integrated circuits
  BT: computer equipment
  NT: LSI
  RT: microprocessors
integrated library systems
  UF: integrated online library systems
  BT: integrated systems
  RT: library automation
integrated online library systems
  USE: integrated library systems
Integrated Services Digital Network
  USE: ISDN
integrated systems
  BT: (hardware, equipment, and
       systems)
  NT: integrated library systems
  RT: computer systems
integration, systems
  USE: systems integration
intellectual freedom
  BT: civil rights
  NT: freedom of information
       freedom to read
  RT: academic freedom
       banned materials
       censorship
intellectual property
  BT: (qualities of information and
       data)
  NT: copyright
       public lending right

intellectual property (cont.)
    RT: legal aspects
           patents
           trade secrets
           trademarks

intelligence
    BT: psychological aspects

intelligent interfaces
    BT: human computer interfaces
    NT: natural language interfaces
    RT: artificial intelligence

interactive design
    USE: computer aided design

interactive systems
    SN: Limit to discussions in which
           interactivity is the primary issue.
           Do not use for all systems which
           happen to be interactive.
    BT: computer systems

interchange formats
    UF: electronic document interchange
           formats
           exchange formats
           information exchange formats
    BT: data formats
    NT: MARC formats
    RT: electronic data interchange

interdisciplinarity
    BT: (qualities of information and
           data)

interfaces
    USE: human computer interfaces

interlibrary cooperation
    USE: cooperation

interlibrary loans
    UF: ILL
    BT: document delivery
           technical services (libraries)
    RT: cooperation
           resource sharing

intermediaries
    USE: online searchers

intermediate index languages
    USE: switching languages

intermediate lexicons
    USE: switching languages

international data flow
    USE: transborder data flow

international librarianship
    BT: librarianship

International Patent Classification
    UF: IPC
    BT: classification schemes

International Standard Book Number
    USE: standard book numbers

International Standard Serial Number
    USE: standard serial numbers

Internet
    BT: telecommunications networks
    RT: listservs
           National Research and Education
           Network

interpretation (linguistic)
    USE: translation

interpreters (linguistic)
    USE: translators

inventory
    BT: management

inverted files
    BT: files

IPC
    USE: International Patent Classification

IRM
    USE: information resources
           management

ISBN
    USE: standard book numbers

ISDN
    UF: Integrated Services Digital
           Network
    BT: telecommunications networks

ISSN
    USE: standard serial numbers

jargon
    BT: languages

journal articles
    USE: periodical articles

journal indexes
    USE: periodical indexes

journals
    SN: Scholarly journals.
    UF: scholarly journals

journals (cont.)
BT: periodicals
NT: electronic journals
RT: periodical articles
primary literature
scholarly publishing

joysticks
BT: input equipment
RT: video games

jukeboxes
SN: For optical disks.
BT: CD-ROM drives
RT: optical discs

key words
USE: keywords

keyboarding
USE: data entry

keyboarding errors
USE: typographical errors

keyboards
BT: input equipment

keying
USE: data entry

keyword in context indexes
USE: KWIC indexes

keyword indexes
UF: natural language indexes
BT: indexes (information retrieval)
NT: concordances
KWIC indexes
KWOC indexes
permuted indexes
RT: keywords

keyword out of context indexes
USE: KWOC indexes

keyword searching
BT: searching
RT: full text searching
keywords

keywords
SN: Terms, frequently single words, used in uncontrolled indexing.
UF: free text indexing
key words
natural language indexing
uncontrolled indexing

keywords (cont.)
BT: index terms
RT: full text databases
keyword indexes
keyword searching
subject headings

knowledge
BT: (by content)
NT: common sense knowledge
concepts
domain knowledge
system knowledge
task knowledge
RT: information
knowledge bases

knowledge acquisition
BT: knowledge engineering
RT: expert systems
knowledge bases
learning

knowledge based systems
USE: knowledge bases

knowledge based systems
USE: expert systems

knowledge bases
UF: frame based systems
knowledge based systems
knowledgebase management systems
knowledgebases
rule based systems
BT: (by medium, physical form)
RT: artificial intelligence
automatic indexing
databases
expert systems
knowledge
knowledge acquisition
knowledge engineering

knowledge engineering
UF: information engineering
BT: (information and library operations)
NT: knowledge acquisition
knowledge representation

knowledge engineering (cont.)
　RT:　expert systems
　　　　knowledge bases
　　　　knowledge representation
knowledge representation
　UF:　data representation
　　　　representation, knowledge
　BT:　knowledge engineering
　RT:　classification
　　　　information processing
　　　　knowledge engineering
knowledge workers
　USE: information workers
knowledgebase management systems
　USE: knowledge bases
knowledgebases
　USE: knowledge bases
known item searching
　BT:　searching
KWIC indexes
　UF:　keyword in context indexes
　BT:　keyword indexes
　RT:　titles
KWOC indexes
　UF:　keyword out of context indexes
　BT:　keyword indexes
　RT:　titles
labor unions
　UF:　unions, labor
　BT:　organizations
LAN
　USE: local area networks
language barriers
　BT:　(sociocultural aspects)
　RT:　foreign languages
language understanding
　USE: natural language understanding
languages
　BT:　(languages)
　NT:　command languages
　　　　context free languages
　　　　English language
　　　　foreign languages
　　　　index languages
　　　　jargon
　　　　markup languages

languages (cont.)
　NT:　programming languages
　　　　query languages
　RT:　idioms
　　　　linguistic analysis
laptop computers
　USE: personal computers
large print materials
　BT:　print materials
　RT:　books
large scale integration
　USE: LSI
laser discs
　USE: optical discs
lasers
　BT:　(hardware, equipment, and
　　　　systems)
　RT:　optical discs
law
　UF:　legislation
　　　　regulations
　BT:　social sciences
　RT:　copyright
　　　　legal aspects
　　　　litigation support
leadership
　BT:　psychological aspects
learning
　BT:　(educational and psychological
　　　　activities)
　NT:　lifelong learning
　　　　machine learning
　　　　perceptual learning
　RT:　knowledge acquisition
learning centers (libraries)
　USE: libraries
learning centers (media centers)
　USE: media centers
learning disabled persons
　UF:　learning handicapped persons
　BT:　disabled persons
learning handicapped persons
　USE: learning disabled persons
learning resource centers
　USE: media centers

leasing, database
    USE: database leasing

legal aspects
    BT: (sociocultural aspects)
    NT: admissibility of records
        legal deposit
        liability
    RT: copyright
        information policy
        intellectual property
        law

legal deposit
    SN: For copyright purposes.
    UF: compulsory deposit
    BT: legal aspects
    RT: copyright

legibility
    BT: (qualities of information and
        data)
    RT: character sets

legislation
    USE: law

lending
    USE: circulation (library)

letter by letter arrangment
    BT: alphabetical arrangement

letters
    USE: correspondence

lexical analysis
    BT: linguistic analysis
    RT: lexicography

lexicography
    BT: humanities
    NT: computational lexicography
    RT: lexical analysis
        thesauri
        words

liability
    BT: legal aspects

liaison agents
    USE: gatekeepers

librarians
    SN: For librarians in specific types of
        libraries, also use the type of
        library, e.g., "special libraries."

librarians (cont.)
    BT: information professionals
        library personnel
    NT: reference librarians
    RT: library associations

librarianship
    SN: Also use the type where appro-
        priate, e.g., "academic libraries."
    UF: library science
    BT: (fields and disciplines)
    NT: comparative librarianship
        international librarianship
    RT: information science
        libraries
        library schools

libraries
    UF: information centers (libraries)
        learning centers (libraries)
    BT: (product and service providers)
    NT: academic libraries
        branch libraries
        central libraries
        children's libraries
        depository libraries
        government libraries
        institutional libraries
        media centers
        mobile libraries
        national libraries
        public libraries
        research libraries
        small libraries
        special libraries
        virtual libraries
    RT: archives
        information infrastructure
        librarianship
        library access
        library associations
        library automation
        library buildings
        library management
        library materials
        library networks
        library services
        problem patrons

library access
BT: access to resources
RT: information access
        libraries
library acquisitions
USE: acquisitions (of materials)
library administration
USE: library management
library assistants
USE: paraprofessional library personnel
library associations
BT: professional associations
RT: librarians
        libraries
library automation
UF: electronic libraries
BT: automation
NT: computerized cataloging
RT: integrated library systems
        libraries
        library services
        virtual libraries
library buildings
BT: buildings
RT: libraries
        library equipment
library collections
UF: book collections
        book stock
        holdings (library)
BT: collections
RT: library materials
library cooperation
USE: cooperation
library education
BT: education
RT: information science education
        library schools
library equipment
BT: (hardware, equipment, and
        systems)
NT: library security systems
        library shelving

library equipment (cont.)
RT: information technology
        library buildings
        library supplies
        storage (materials)
library extension
USE: outreach services (library)
library instruction
USE: bibliographic instruction
library management
UF: library administration
BT: management
RT: information resources
        management
        libraries
library materials
BT: (by information content, purpose)
NT: overdue materials
RT: banned materials
        collection management
        libraries
        library collections
library networks
UF: library systems
BT: networks
RT: academic libraries
        cooperation
        libraries
        telecommunications networks
Library of Congress Classification
BT: classification schemes
Library of Congress Subject Headings
BT: subject heading lists
library patrons
USE: library users
library patrons
USE: users
library personnel
UF: library staff
BT: information workers
NT: librarians
        paraprofessional library personnel
RT: media specialists
library programs
UF: adult programs
BT: library services

library schools
    BT: colleges and universities
    RT: librarianship
           library education
library science
    USE: librarianship
library security systems
    UF: theft detection systems
    BT: library equipment
library services
    BT: (information and library
           operations)
    NT: children's services
           library programs
           off campus library services
           outreach services (library)
           reader services
           reference services
           technical services (libraries)
           young adult services
    RT: information services
           libraries
           library automation
           storytelling
library shelving
    UF: compact shelving
           library stacks
           movable shelving
           rolling stacks
           shelving, library
    BT: library equipment
    RT: storage (materials)
library skills
    BT: (human qualities)
    NT: reference skills
    RT: bibliographic instruction
library stacks
    USE: library shelving
library staff
    USE: library personnel
library suppliers
    BT: (product and service providers)
library supplies
    BT: (hardware, equipment, and
           systems)
    RT: library equipment

library support staff
    USE: paraprofessional library personnel
library surveys
    BT: surveys
    RT: user studies
library systems
    USE: library networks
library technical assistants
    USE: paraprofessional library personnel
library technicians
    USE: paraprofessional library personnel
library use
    USE: information use
library user services
    USE: reader services
library users
    UF: borrowers
           library patrons
           patrons, library
    BT: users
    NT: problem patrons
    RT: information use
library weeks
    BT: promotion
lifelong learning
    BT: learning
    RT: adult education
           continuing education
           distance learning
light pens
    UF: light wands
    BT: input equipment
light wands
    USE: light pens
limited area networks
    USE: local area networks
limited cataloging
    USE: minimal cataloging
linear programming
    UF: linear systems
    BT: mathematical methods
linear systems
    USE: linear programming

linguistic analysis
- BT: text processing
- NT: disambiguation
  lexical analysis
  morphological analysis
  semantic analysis
  syntactic analysis
- RT: languages
  linguistics

linguistics
- BT: humanities
- NT: computational linguistics
  etymology
  grammars
  phonetics
  semiotics
- RT: information science
  linguistic analysis

links (between indexing terms)
- SN: Indications that two index terms assigned to the same document are connected in some way.
- BT: (knowledge and information organization devices)
- RT: index languages
  postcoordinate indexing
  role indicators
  subject indexing

links (hypermedia)
- USE: index languages

links (hypertext)
- UF: hypertext links
- BT: access points
- RT: hypertext

listservs
- SN: Services available on networks such as the Internet, to which subscribers may send communications for distribution to all other subscribers to the listserv.
- BT: message systems
- RT: Internet

literacy
- SN: The ability to read and write; for the ability to use information effectively use "information literacy"; for the ability to use computers use "computer literacy."
- UF: adult literacy
  functional literacy
  illiteracy
- BT: (sociocultural aspects)
- RT: information literacy

literacy, computer
- USE: computer literacy

literacy, information
- USE: information literacy

literary reviews
- USE: book reviews

literary warrant
- BT: (qualities of information and data)
- RT: index language construction
  indexing
  vocabulary control

literature
- SN: Belles-lettres.
- BT: (by content)
  humanities
- NT: fiction
  poetry

literature reviews
- SN: More or less comprehensive reviews of the literature of a field.
- UF: reviews of the literature
- BT: reviews

litigation support
- BT: information services
- RT: law

loans
- USE: circulation (library)

local area networks
- UF: LAN
  limited area networks
  local networks
- BT: telecommunications networks

local area networks (cont.)
    RT: file servers
          office automation
local networks
    USE: local area networks
locators
    SN: Devices which indicate the
          position of information items
          within files.
    UF: page references
          reference locators
    BT: (knowledge and information
          organization devices)
logic
    BT: humanities
    NT: Boolean logic
          predicate logic
          propositional logic
    RT: logic programming
          logical skills
          mathematics
logic programming
    BT: computer programming
    RT: logic
logical operators
    USE: Boolean logic
logical skills
    BT: (human qualities)
    RT: logic
long term memory
    BT: memory (human)
look and feel
    SN: Of an interface.
    BT: (qualities of systems and
          equipment)
    RT: human computer interfaces
loose leaf services
    BT: reference materials
Lotka's law
    SN: A rule relating the number of
          occurrences of authors' names in
          a bibliographic database to the
          number of different authors found
          in the database.
    BT: bibliometrics

LSI
    UF: large scale integration
    BT: integrated circuits
    NT: VLSI
LTAs
    USE: paraprofessional library personnel
machine aided translation
    USE: machine translation
machine learning
    UF: computer learning
    BT: artificial intelligence
          learning
    NT: font learning
machine readable cataloguing formats
    USE: MARC formats
machine readable cataloguing records
    USE: MARC records
machine readable data
    SN: Limit to information emphasizing
          the aspect of machine readability,
          and also use a term for the
          specific kind of information, e.g.,
          "dictionaries."
    BT: data
machine readable files
    USE: files
machine readable records
    USE: records
machine translation
    UF: automatic translation
          computer aided translation
          computer translation
          machine aided translation
          MT
    BT: translation
machine vision
    USE: computer vision
magazines
    USE: periodicals
magnetic disks
    BT: disks
          magnetic media
    NT: floppy disks
          hard disks
          magneto-optical disks

magnetic media
- BT: (physical media)
- NT: magnetic disks
  - magnetic tapes

magnetic recording
- BT: recording

magnetic resonance imaging
- UF: MRI
- BT: imaging

magnetic tapes
- BT: magnetic media
- NT: audiotapes

magneto-optical disks
- BT: magnetic disks
  - optical discs

main libraries
- USE: central libraries

mainframe computers
- BT: computers

maintainability
- BT: (qualities of systems and equipment)
- RT: durability
  - maintenance
  - quality
  - reliability

maintenance
- BT: (general activities)
- NT: database maintenance
  - thesaurus maintenance
  - updating
- RT: maintainability

man machine interfaces
- USE: human computer interfaces

management
- UF: administration
- BT: (business and management operations)
- NT: computing resource management
  - critical incident method
  - critical path method
  - financial management
  - human resource management
  - information resources management

management (cont.)
- NT: inventory
  - library management
- RT: decision support systems
  - management information systems
  - managers
  - organization charts
  - planning
  - scheduling

management communications
- USE: management information systems

management information systems
- UF: management communications
  - MIS
- BT: information retrieval systems
- RT: decision support systems
  - executive information systems
  - management

managers
- BT: (persons and informal groups)
- RT: management

manual indexing
- UF: human indexing
- BT: indexing

manuscripts
- BT: (by medium, physical form)
- RT: archives
  - rare materials

mapping (cartography)
- USE: cartography

mapping (graphic representation)
- BT: (knowledge and information organization devices)

mapping (sets)
- BT: set theory

maps
- BT: (by medium, physical form)
- RT: cartography
  - visual materials

MARC formats
- UF: machine readable cataloguing formats
- BT: interchange formats
- RT: MARC records

MARC records
UF: machine readable cataloguing records
BT: bibliographic records
RT: MARC formats

marginalia
BT: (by information content, purpose)

marketing
BT: (business and management operations)
NT: advertising
promotion
telemarketing
RT: focus groups
promotion
public relations

Markov chains
USE: Markov models

Markov models
SN: Models in which the probabilities of future events depend only on the current state of the model, and not on how the model got to that state.
UF: Markov chains
Markov processes
BT: mathematical models

Markov processes
USE: Markov models

markup languages
BT: languages
RT: editing

mass communications
USE: mass media

mass media
UF: mass communications
BT: (communications media)
NT: newspapers
radio
television

massively parallel processing
USE: parallel processing

mathematical methods
BT: (research and analytic methods)
NT: factor analysis
finite element analysis

mathematical methods (cont.)
NT: Fourier analysis
game theory
graph theory
Hough transformation
linear programming
nonlinear programming
set theory
statistical methods
vector analysis
RT: mathematics

mathematical models
BT: models
NT: Markov models
stochastic models

mathematics
SN: The discipline; for applications in research and analysis, use "mathematical methods."
BT: (fields and disciplines)
NT: operations research
RT: game theory
graph theory
logic
mathematical methods
set theory
statistical methods

matrices
BT: (knowledge and information organization devices)

meaning
USE: semantics

measurement
BT: (research and analytic methods)
NT: econometrics
infometrics
photogrammetry
psychometrics
RT: remote sensing

media
SN: Use the specific kind of medium, e.g., "journals," "books," "films."
BT: (by medium, physical form)

media centers
UF: learning centers (media centers)
　　 learning resource centers
　　 resource centers
　　 school libraries
　　 school media centers
BT: libraries
media instruction
USE: bibliographic instruction
media materials
USE: nonprint media
media specialists
BT: information professionals
RT: library personnel
mediated searching
USE: online searchers
medical informatics
UF: informatics, medical
BT: informatics
RT: medical records
　　 medicine
　　 tomography
medical records
BT: records
RT: confidential records
　　 medical informatics
medicine
BT: biomedical sciences
RT: medical informatics
　　 pharmacology
meetings
UF: conferences
BT: face to face communications
NT: workshops
RT: face to face communications
　　 oral communications
　　 workshops
memoranda
USE: correspondence
memory (computer)
UF: computer memory
BT: computers
NT: associative memory
　　 content addressable memory
　　 holographic memory
　　 random access memory

memory (computer) (cont.)
NT: read only memory
　　 virtual memory
memory (human)
BT: (natural functions and events)
NT: long term memory
　　 short term memory
　　 visual memory
mental models
USE: cognitive models
mental processes
BT: (natural functions and events)
NT: abstraction
　　 cognition
　　 comprehension
　　 generalization
　　 perception (conceptual)
　　 perception (sensory)
　　 reasoning
　　 serendipity
　　 visualization
menu based interfaces
UF: menus
BT: human computer interfaces
menus
USE: menu based interfaces
message systems
UF: messaging systems
BT: computer mediated
　　 communications
NT: bulletin board systems
　　 electronic mail
　　 listservs
　　 voice mail
messaging systems
USE: message systems
metaphors
UF: analogies
BT: information representations
NT: desktop metaphor
metropolitan area networks
BT: telecommunications networks
mice (computer peripherals)
UF: mouse (computer peripheral)
BT: pointing devices

mice (computer peripherals) (cont.)
RT: graphical user interfaces
trackballs (computer peripherals)

microcomputers
SN: Computers built around
microprocessors on integrated
circuit chips. For microcomputers
designed for individual desktop or
travel use, use "personal
computers."
BT: computers
NT: personal computers
RT: microprocessors

microfiche
BT: microforms

microfilm
BT: microforms
RT: computer output microform

microforms
UF: micrographics
BT: (physical media)
NT: computer output microform
microfiche
microfilm
RT: micropublishing

micrographics
USE: microforms

microprocessing
USE: microprocessors

microprocessors
UF: microprocessing
microtechnology
BT: processing units (computers)
RT: integrated circuits
microcomputers

microproduction
USE: micropublishing

microprograms
BT: computer software

micropublishing
UF: microproduction
BT: publishing
RT: microforms

microtechnology
USE: microprocessors

microthesauri
SN: Thesauri which are subsets,
usually limited to a specialized
topic, of larger thesauri.
UF: minithesauri
BT: thesauri

minicomputers
BT: computers
NT: superminicomputers

minimal cataloging
UF: limited cataloging
BT: cataloging (bibliographic)

minithesauri
USE: microthesauri

MIS
USE: management information systems

mission oriented research
BT: research and development

misspellings
USE: typographical errors

mixed media
USE: multimedia

mobile communications
BT: telecommunications
NT: cellular communications

mobile libraries
BT: libraries
NT: bookmobiles

mobile telephones
USE: cellular communications

modeling
USE: models

models
UF: modeling
BT: (research and analytic methods)
NT: connectionist models
database models
hierarchical models
information models
mathematical models
predictive models
user models
vector space models
RT: operations research
simulation

modems
- BT: telecommunications equipment
- RT: transmission speed

modifiers
- SN: Terms or phrases, usually applied ad hoc, which differentiate among the entries under a main term in an index entry.
- UF: subdivisions (indexing)
  subheadings
- BT: index terms

modularity
- BT: (qualities of systems and equipment)
- RT: computer programming
  systems design

monitoring
- UF: surveillance
- BT: (general activities)
- RT: evaluation

monographs
- BT: publications
- RT: books
  primary literature
  scholarly publishing

Monte Carlo method
- BT: statistical methods
- RT: probability

morphological analysis
- BT: linguistic analysis

motion pictures
- USE: films

motion video
- UF: full motion video
- BT: video recordings

motivation
- BT: psychological aspects

mouse (computer peripheral)
- USE: mice (computer peripherals)

movable shelving
- USE: library shelving

moving
- BT: (business and management operations)
- RT: storage (materials)

MRI
- USE: magnetic resonance imaging

MT
- USE: machine translation

multi database searching
- USE: crossfile searching

multilingual subject indexing
- BT: subject indexing
- RT: foreign languages
  multilingual thesauri

multilingual thesauri
- BT: thesauri
- RT: foreign language materials
  foreign languages
  multilingual subject indexing

multimedia
- UF: mixed media
- BT: (by medium, physical form)

multiple access communications
- BT: telecommunications

multiplexing
- SN: Transmission of several lower-speed data streams simultaneously over a single higher-speed line.
- BT: telecommunications

multiprocessing
- BT: data processing
- RT: multiprocessors

multiprocessors
- BT: processing units (computers)
- RT: multiprocessing

multitasking
- BT: data processing

multivariate analysis
- BT: statistical methods

municipal libraries
- USE: public libraries

museum informatics
- UF: informatics, museum
- BT: informatics
- RT: museums

museums
- BT: (product and service providers)
- RT: museum informatics

music
>   BT: (by content)
>   fine arts

name indexing
>   UF: corporate name indexing
>   personal name indexing
>   BT: indexing
>   RT: identifiers
>   personal names

names
>   USE: proper names

narrower term references
>   USE: cross references

narrower term relationships
>   USE: hierarchical relationships

national bibliographies
>   BT: bibliographies

national libraries
>   BT: libraries

National Research and Education Network
>   UF: NREN
>   BT: telecommunications networks
>   RT: Internet

natural language indexes
>   USE: keyword indexes

natural language indexing
>   USE: keywords

natural language interfaces
>   BT: intelligent interfaces

natural language processing
>   UF: NLP
>   BT: artificial intelligence
>   NT: discourse analysis
>   discourse generation
>   natural language understanding
>   sentence generation
>   speech recognition
>   speech synthesis
>   RT: automatic indexing
>   full text searching
>   information retrieval
>   natural language searching
>   probabilistic indexing
>   relevance ranking
>   text processing

natural language searching
>   BT: searching
>   RT: natural language processing

natural language understanding
>   UF: language understanding
>   understanding (natural language)
>   BT: natural language processing

natural sciences
>   BT: (fields and disciplines)
>   NT: biomedical sciences
>   earth sciences
>   ecology
>   geography

navigation
>   SN: Of information retrieval systems.
>   BT: (information and library
>   operations)
>   RT: human computer interfaces
>   searching

near-published literature
>   USE: grey literature

near-synonymous relationships
>   USE: quasi-synonymous relationships

needs assessment
>   UF: assessment, needs
>   BT: (research and analytic methods)
>   RT: information needs

negotiation
>   BT: communications

network analysis
>   BT: (research and analytic methods)

network protocols
>   USE: communications protocols

network servers
>   USE: file servers

networking
>   USE: personal networking

networks
>   SN: Very broad term; prefer specific
>   type, e.g., "library networks."
>   BT: (networks)
>   NT: library networks
>   neural networks
>   nodes
>   semantic networks
>   telecommunications networks

networks (cont.)
    RT: personal networking
           spreading activation
neural nets
    USE: neural networks
neural networks
    UF: neural nets
    BT: artificial intelligence
           networks
    RT: spreading activation
news
    BT: (by content)
    RT: newsletters
           newspapers
           newswire services
news wire services
    USE: newswire services
newsletters
    BT: periodicals
    RT: news
newspapers
    BT: mass media
           serials
    RT: news
newswire services
    UF: news wire services
           wire services
    BT: publishers
    RT: news
NLP
    USE: natural language processing
nodes
    BT: networks
noise (acoustic)
    BT: sound
noise (information retrieval)
    UF: false drops
    BT: (qualities of information and
           data)
    RT: evaluation
           fallout
           precision
           recall
           relevance
           retrieval effectiveness

nomenclature
    USE: terminology
nonbibliographic databases
    BT: databases
    NT: community resource files
           fact databases
           human resource files
           image databases
nonfiction
    BT: (by content)
    RT: books
nonhierarchical relationships
    USE: associative relationships
nonlinear programming
    BT: mathematical methods
nonpreferred term references
    USE: cross references
nonprint media
    UF: audio-visual materials
           audiovisual aids
           audiovisual materials
           media materials
    BT: (by medium, physical form)
    NT: sound recordings
           visual materials
    RT: hypermedia
nonprofessional library personnel
    USE: paraprofessional library personnel
nonroman scripts
    BT: writing systems
nonverbal communications
    BT: face to face communications
normalization
    BT: data processing
    RT: data models
notation
    BT: information representations
    RT: classification
           classification schemes
           notation synthesis
notation synthesis
    UF: synthesis, notation
    BT: classification
    RT: notation
notebook computers
    USE: personal computers

nothing before something arrangement
    USE: word by word arrangement
novels
    USE: fiction
novice users
    BT: end users
NREN
    USE: National Research and Education
          Network
NT references
    USE: cross references
NT relationships
    USE: hierarchical relationships
numeric data
    BT: data
    RT: numeric databases
          spreadsheets
numeric databases
    UF: data banks
          data sets
          databanks
          statistical databases
    BT: fact databases
    RT: numeric data
numeric range searching
    USE: range searching
object oriented databases
    BT: databases
    RT: object oriented programming
          objects (data structures)
object oriented programming
    UF: OOP
    BT: computer programming
    RT: object oriented databases
          objects (data structures)
object recognition
    BT: pattern recognition
objectives
    USE: goals
objects (data structures)
    SN: Self-contained entities that
          incorporate both their properties
          and the operations to be
          performed on the entities.
    BT: abstract data types

objects (data structures) (cont.)
    RT: object oriented databases
          object oriented programming
objects (physical)
    USE: physical objects
obscene materials
    USE: pornographic materials
obsolescence
    BT: (general qualities)
    RT: aging of literatures
          information life cycle
OCR
    USE: optical character recognition
off campus education
    UF: extension campuses
    BT: education
    RT: adult education
          distance learning
off campus library services
    BT: library services
off site access
    USE: remote access
office automation
    UF: electronic offices
    BT: automation
    RT: local area networks
offsite access
    USE: remote access
one person libraries
    USE: small libraries
online catalogs
    USE: OPACs
online computing
    BT: (computer operations)
    NT: online searching
online databases
    BT: databases
    NT: OPACs
    RT: online searching
online industry
    BT: information industry
    RT: database producers
          information utilities
          online searchers
          online searching
          search services

online information retrieval
USE: online searching
online information retrieval systems
USE: information retrieval systems
online public access catalogs
USE: OPACs

online searchers
SN: Individuals who perform searchers on behalf of others; for individuals searching for their own needs, use "end users."
UF: intermediaries
mediated searching
search intermediaries
searchers
BT: information professionals
RT: information brokers
online industry
online searching
presearch interviews
reference librarians
search behavior

online searching
UF: online information retrieval
BT: online computing
searching
NT: crossfile searching
RT: downloading
full text searching
information retrieval systems
online databases
online industry
online searchers
retrieval software
search strategies
online systems
USE: information retrieval systems

online...
SN: Use "online..."
BT: (computer operations)

OOP
USE: object oriented programming

OPACs
UF: online catalogs
online public access catalogs

OPACs (cont.)
BT: bibliographic databases
catalogs (bibliographic)
online databases

operating systems
BT: computer software

operations research
BT: mathematics
RT: models
optimization

operators, logical
USE: Boolean logic

optical character recognition
UF: character recognition
OCR
BT: optical recognition
NT: feature extraction
font learning
RT: pattern recognition

optical computers
BT: computers
optical equipment

optical discs
UF: laser discs
BT: disks
optical media
NT: compact discs
erasable optical discs
floptical discs
magneto-optical disks
videodiscs
WORM discs
RT: jukeboxes
lasers

optical equipment
BT: (hardware, equipment, and systems)
NT: optical computers
optical media
RT: floptical discs
optical recording
optical tape
optoelectronic computers
optical fibers
USE: fiber optics

optical media
BT: (physical media)
optical equipment
NT: optical discs
optical tape
RT: optical recording

optical recognition
BT: pattern recognition
NT: optical character recognition
RT: bar codes
scanning

optical recording
BT: recording
RT: optical equipment
optical media

optical scanners
USE: scanners

optical scanning
USE: scanning

optical tape
BT: optical media
RT: optical equipment

optimization
BT: (research and analytic methods)
RT: operations research

optoelectronic computers
BT: computers
RT: optical equipment

oral communications
BT: communications
NT: presearch interviews
reference interviews
RT: face to face communications
informal communications
meetings

oral history
BT: (by content)

ordering (materials)
BT: acquisitions (of materials)
NT: blanket orders
standing orders

organization charts
BT: (by medium, physical form)
RT: management

organization names
USE: corporate names

organization of information
BT: (information and library
operations)
NT: cataloging (bibliographic)
classification
database design
facet analysis
index language construction
indexing
relevance ranking
subject analysis

organization theory
BT: sociology

organizational communications
BT: communications
RT: informal communications
organizational culture
organizational environment
personal networking

organizational culture
UF: corporate culture
BT: (sociocultural aspects)
RT: organizational communications
organizational environment

organizational environment
BT: (sociocultural aspects)
RT: organizational communications
organizational culture

organizations
BT: (organizations)
NT: armed forces
consortia
friends of libraries
labor unions
professional associations

out of print publications
BT: publications
RT: rare materials

output equipment
BT: computer peripherals
NT: printers (equipment)
RT: video display terminals

output reformatting
BT: (information and library
operations)

outreach services (library)
  UF: community based library services
        library extension
  BT: library services

overdue materials
  BT: library materials
  RT: circulation (library)

overhead costs
  BT: costs

overlap
  SN: In scope or coverage.
  BT: (qualities of information and
        data)

overload, information
  USE: information overload

packet switching
  BT: telecommunications

page references
  USE: locators

palmtop computers
  USE: personal computers

paper
  BT: (physical media)

paper based information systems
  BT: information retrieval systems

paperbacks
  BT: books

paperwork management
  USE: records management

paradigms
  BT: (knowledge and information
        organization devices)

parallel architecture
  USE: parallel processors

parallel processing
  UF: concurrent processing
        massively parallel processing
  BT: data processing
  RT: parallel processors

parallel processors
  UF: parallel architecture
  BT: processing units (computers)
  RT: parallel processing

paraprofessional library personnel
  UF: library assistants
        library support staff

paraprofessional library personnel (cont.)
  UF: library technical assistants
        library technicians
        LTAs
        nonprofessional library personnel
        support staff, library
  BT: library personnel

parsing
  USE: syntactic analysis

part whole relationships
  BT: hierarchical relationships
  RT: cross references
        hierarchical relationships

partial match retrieval systems
  USE: fuzzy retrieval systems

participative problem solving
  BT: problem solving

patents
  SN: Use for information about
        patents, not for examples of
        patents.
  BT: (by information content, purpose)
  RT: innovation
        intellectual property

patrons
  USE: users

patrons, library
  USE: library users

pattern matching
  USE: pattern recognition

pattern recognition
  UF: pattern matching
  BT: data processing
  NT: object recognition
        optical recognition
        word recognition
  RT: optical character recognition

pay per view television
  BT: television

PC
  USE: personal computers

peer review
  USE: refereeing

pen based computing
  UF: handwritten input
  BT: (computer operations)

perception (conceptual)
　　BT:　mental processes
perception (sensory)
　　UF:　sensory perception
　　　　　tactile sensations
　　BT:　mental processes
　　RT:　perceptual learning
perceptual learning
　　BT:　learning
　　RT:　perception (sensory)
performance
　　BT:　(general qualities)
　　RT:　costs
　　　　　durability
　　　　　effectiveness
　　　　　quality
　　　　　reliability
　　　　　response time
　　　　　search time
performing arts
　　BT:　(fields and disciplines)
periodical articles
　　UF:　articles, periodical
　　　　　journal articles
　　BT:　periodicals
　　RT:　journals
periodical indexes
　　UF:　journal indexes
　　BT:　indexes (information retrieval)
　　RT:　abstracting and indexing services
　　　　　databases
periodical indexing
　　BT:　indexing
　　RT:　database indexing
periodicals
　　UF:　magazines
　　BT:　serials
　　NT:　journals
　　　　　newsletters
　　　　　periodical articles
peripherals, computer
　　USE: computer peripherals

permanence
　　BT:　(general qualities)
　　RT:　durability
　　　　　quality
　　　　　reliability
permuted indexes
　　UF:　rotated indexes
　　BT:　keyword indexes
personal collections
　　BT:　collections
　　RT:　personal files
personal computers
　　SN:　Microcomputers intended for
　　　　　individual desktop or travel use.
　　UF:　desktop computers
　　　　　laptop computers
　　　　　notebook computers
　　　　　palmtop computers
　　　　　PC
　　BT:　microcomputers
personal data
　　SN:　Data and information about
　　　　　individual persons.
　　BT:　data
　　RT:　data security
　　　　　privacy
personal files
　　BT:　files
　　RT:　personal collections
personal name indexing
　　USE: name indexing
personal names
　　UF:　forenames
　　　　　surnames
　　BT:　proper names
　　RT:　authority files
　　　　　name indexing
personal networking
　　SN:　Personal networking; for networks
　　　　　of organizations or equipment,
　　　　　use "networks" or the
　　　　　appropriate specific term, e.g.,
　　　　　"computer networks."
　　UF:　networking
　　BT:　communications

personal networking (cont.)
  RT: gatekeepers
       human information sources
       information filtering
       information flow
       information seeking
       networks
       organizational communications
personnel
  USE: employees
pharmacology
  UF: drugs
  BT: biomedical sciences
  RT: chemistry
       medicine
philosophy
  BT: humanities
phonetics
  BT: linguistics
photocopiers
  UF: copiers
  BT: (hardware, equipment, and
       systems)
  RT: photocopying
photocopying
  UF: copying
  BT: (information and library
       operations)
  RT: photocopiers
photogrammetry
  BT: measurement
  RT: remote sensing
photographic films
  BT: (physical media)
photographs
  BT: images
phrases
  BT: (linguistic elements)
physical location
  UF: geographic location
  BT: (general qualities)
physical objects
  UF: objects (physical)
  BT: (by medium, physical form)

physical sciences
  BT: (fields and disciplines)
  NT: chemistry
       physics
physically challenged persons
  USE: disabled persons
physicians
  BT: (persons and informal groups)
  RT: biomedical sciences
physics
  BT: physical sciences
pictorial information systems
  USE: image information systems
picture telephones
  USE: videotelephones
planning
  BT: (business and management
       operations)
  NT: strategic planning
  RT: forecasting
       goals
       management
       scheduling
poetry
  BT: literature
pointing devices
  BT: input equipment
  NT: mice (computer peripherals)
       trackballs (computer peripherals)
policy, public
  USE: public policy
political science
  BT: social sciences
politics
  BT: (sociocultural aspects)
  RT: information policy
popular materials
  BT: (by information content, purpose)
pornographic materials
  UF: indecent materials
       obscene materials
  BT: (by information content, purpose)
  RT: erotic materials
postcoordinate indexing
  UF: coordinate indexing
  BT: subject indexing

postcoordinate indexing (cont.)
    RT: links (between indexing terms)
           role indicators

pragmatics
    BT: semiotics

PRECIS
    UF: Preserved Context Indexing
           System
    BT: subject indexing

precision
    SN: The percentage of relevant
           documents in a retrieved set.
    BT: (qualities of information and
           data)
    RT: fallout
           noise (information retrieval)
           recall
           retrieval effectiveness

precoordinate indexing
    BT: subject indexing

predicate calculus
    USE: predicate logic

predicate logic
    UF: predicate calculus
    BT: logic

prediction
    USE: forecasting

predictive models
    BT: models

preferred order
    USE: citation order

preferred term references
    USE: cross references

preprints
    SN: Use for information about
           preprints, not for examples of
           preprints.
    BT: grey literature

presearch interviews
    BT: oral communications
    RT: online searchers

preservation of library materials
    BT: (information and library
           operations)

preservation of library materials (cont.)
    NT: binding
           conservation of library materials
           restoration
    RT: technical services (libraries)

Preserved Context Indexing System
    USE: PRECIS

Presidential libraries
    BT: research libraries
           special libraries

prices
    USE: pricing

pricing
    UF: charges
           fees
           prices
    BT: (business and management
           operations)
    NT: fees for service
           royalties

primary literature
    BT: (by information content, purpose)
    RT: journals
           monographs

print materials
    BT: publications
    NT: large print materials

printers (equipment)
    BT: output equipment

printing
    BT: (technical and manufacturing
           operations)
    RT: publishing

privacy
    UF: confidentiality
    BT: civil rights
    RT: confidential records
           data security
           disclosure
           information policy
           personal data
           security

private sector
    BT: (sectors of the economy)
    RT: competition

probabilistic indexing
    BT: indexing
    RT: associative retrieval
         natural language processing
         probabilistic retrieval
         probability

probabilistic retrieval
    UF: statistical retrieval
    BT: information retrieval
    RT: associative retrieval
         probabilistic indexing
         probability
         relevance ranking

probability
    BT: (general qualities)
    RT: Bayesian functions
         Monte Carlo method
         probabilistic indexing
         probabilistic retrieval
         queuing
         statistical methods
         stochastic processes
         uncertainty

problem patrons
    UF: problem users
    BT: library users
    RT: libraries

problem solving
    BT: (research and analytic methods)
    NT: heuristics
         participative problem solving

problem users
    USE: problem patrons

processing units (computers)
    UF: central processing units
         CPU
         data processors
    BT: computers
    NT: array processors
         back end processors
         microprocessors
         multiprocessors
         parallel processors

productivity
    BT: (human qualities)

professional associations
    UF: associations
         professional societies
         scientific societies
         societies
    BT: organizations
    NT: information associations
         library associations

professional societies
    USE: professional associations

professionals
    USE: information professionals

programming (computer)
    USE: computer programming

programming languages
    UF: computer languages
    BT: languages
    NT: high level languages
    RT: computer programming
         computer software

programs, computer
    USE: computer software

promotion
    BT: marketing
    NT: library weeks
    RT: marketing

proofreading
    BT: text processing
    RT: editing
         publishing

proper names
    UF: names
    BT: (by content)
    NT: corporate names
         personal names
    RT: authority files

propositional logic
    BT: logic

protocols
    USE: communications protocols

prototypes
    USE: prototyping

prototyping
    UF: prototypes
    BT: testing

proximity searching
UF: adjacency searching
BT: searching
RT: string searching

psychological aspects
SN: Of information and information use. For the discipline use "psychology."
BT: (sociocultural aspects)
NT: attitudes
       intelligence
       leadership
       motivation
RT: human behavior

psychology
SN: The discipline; for applications to information use, use "psychological aspects."
BT: behavioral sciences
NT: psychometrics
       social psychology
RT: human behavior

psychometrics
BT: measurement
       psychology

public domain software
BT: computer software

public information
BT: information
RT: public records

public lending right
BT: intellectual property
RT: copyright
       royalties

public libraries
UF: municipal libraries
BT: libraries
RT: branch libraries
       research libraries
       state library agencies

public policy
UF: government policy
       policy, public
BT: (sociocultural aspects)
NT: information policy

public records
BT: records
RT: freedom of information
       public information

public relations
BT: communications
RT: marketing

public sector
BT: (sectors of the economy)
RT: government agencies

publication explosion
USE: information explosion

publications
SN: Very general term. Prefer specific type, e.g., "journals," "books."
UF: information products
BT: (by availability, access, organization)
NT: alternative publications
       books
       electronic publications
       government publications
       monographs
       out of print publications
       print materials
       serials
       series
RT: publishing

publishers
BT: (product and service providers)
NT: database producers
       newswire services
       small presses
RT: information industry
       information infrastructure
       publishing

publishing
BT: communications
NT: desktop publishing
       electronic publishing
       micropublishing
       scholarly publishing
RT: information explosion
       information production
       printing

publishing (cont.)
  RT: proofreading
       publications
       publishers
       software industry

QBE
  USE: query by example

qualifiers
  SN: Delimiters used to distinguish
       different meanings of words or
       terms which are spelled the same.
  BT: index terms

qualitative research
  BT: research and development

quality
  BT: (general qualities)
  RT: evaluation
       maintainability
       performance
       permanence
       quality assurance
       quality control

quality assurance
  BT: (technical and manufacturing
       operations)
  RT: quality
       quality control

quality control
  BT: (technical and manufacturing
       operations)
  NT: duplicate detection
       error correction
       error detection
  RT: evaluation
       quality
       quality assurance

quasi-synonymous relationships
  UF: near-synonymous relationships
  BT: equivalence relationships

query by example
  UF: QBE
  BT: searching

query expansion
  BT: query refinement

query formulation
  UF: search formulation
  BT: searching

query languages
  BT: languages
  NT: structured query languages
  RT: query processing

query processing
  BT: information processing
  RT: query languages

query refinement
  BT: searching
  NT: query expansion

query weighting
  USE: weighting

question answering retrieval
  USE: answer passage retrieval

question answering systems
  USE: fact retrieval systems

questionnaires
  USE: surveys

queuing
  BT: stochastic processes
  RT: probability

radiation
  BT: (natural functions and events)

radio
  BT: mass media
  RT: broadcasting

RAM
  USE: random access memory

random access memory
  UF: RAM
  BT: memory (computer)
  NT: DRAM

random processes
  USE: stochastic processes

range searching
  UF: numeric range searching
  BT: searching

ranking (relevance)
  USE: relevance ranking

rare materials
  UF: antiquarian materials
  BT: (by availability, access,
       organization)

rare materials (cont.)
   RT: archives
       manuscripts
       out of print publications
       special collections
read only memory
   UF: ROM
   BT: memory (computer)
reader services
   UF: library user services
       reading guidance
   BT: library services
   RT: circulation (library)
       reference services
reading
   BT: communications
   RT: bibliotherapy
       education
reading disabled persons
   UF: dyslexia
       reading handicapped persons
   BT: disabled persons
reading guidance
   USE: reader services
reading handicapped persons
   USE: reading disabled persons
ready reference materials
   BT: reference materials
real time processing
   BT: data processing
realia
   BT: visual materials
reasoning
   BT: mental processes
   NT: inference
recall
   SN: The ratio of the relevant
       documents retrieved by a query to
       the total number of relevant
       documents in the system.
   BT: (qualities of information and
       data)
   RT: evaluation
       fallout

recall (cont.)
   RT: noise (information retrieval)
       precision
       retrieval effectiveness
recording
   BT: (technical and manufacturing
       operations)
   NT: magnetic recording
       optical recording
recordings, sound
   USE: sound recordings
records
   SN: Collections of information items,
       each collection referring to a
       particular entity. For video or
       sound recordings, use recordings.
   UF: machine readable records
   BT: (by information content, purpose)
   NT: administrative records
       bibliographic records
       confidential records
       duplicate records
       medical records
       public records
   RT: data
       films
       records management
records handling
   USE: records management
records management
   UF: paperwork management
       records handling
   BT: information resources
       management
   NT: retention of documents
   RT: archives
       collection management
       correspondence
       information resources
       management
       records
       records managers
       storage (materials)
records managers
   BT: information professionals
   RT: records management

reduced instruction set computers
USE: RISC

refereeing
UF: peer review
BT: evaluation

reference interviews
BT: oral communications
reference services

reference librarians
BT: librarians
RT: online searchers
reference services

reference locators
USE: locators

reference materials
BT: (by information content, purpose)
NT: almanacs
dictionaries
directories
encyclopedias
handbooks
loose leaf services
ready reference materials
yearbooks

reference retrieval systems
UF: bibliographic retrieval systems
BT: information retrieval systems
RT: bibliographic databases

reference services
BT: library services
NT: reference interviews
RT: reader services
reference librarians

reference skills
BT: library skills

referral services
USE: community information services

regulations
USE: law

related term references
USE: cross references

related term relationships
USE: associative relationships

relational databases
BT: databases

relational models
BT: database models

relevance
SN: Applicability of retrieved documents or information to the subject of a query.
BT: (qualities of information and data)
RT: evaluation
fallout
information retrieval systems
noise (information retrieval)
relevance judgments
relevance ranking
retrieval effectiveness
similarity

relevance judgments
BT: (information and library operations)
RT: evaluation
information retrieval
relevance

relevance ranking
UF: closest match
ranking (relevance)
BT: organization of information
RT: fuzzy retrieval systems
natural language processing
probabilistic retrieval
relevance

reliability
BT: (general qualities)
RT: complexity
data corruption
durability
error correction
error detection
error rates
errors
fault tolerance
file integrity
indexer consistency
maintainability
performance
permanence

remote access
SN: To information systems.
UF: off site access
offsite access
BT: access to resources

remote control
BT: control systems
NT: telerobotics

remote sensing
BT: (research and analytic methods)
RT: measurement
photogrammetry
telemetry

reports, technical
USE: technical reports

representation, knowledge
USE: knowledge representation

representations, document
USE: document surrogates

research and development
BT: (research and analytic methods)
NT: empirical studies
mission oriented research
qualitative research
research methods
RT: evaluation
testing

research libraries
BT: libraries
NT: Presidential libraries
RT: academic libraries
public libraries

research methods
BT: research and development

resource centers
USE: media centers

resource management (computing)
USE: computing resource management

resource management (information)
USE: information resources
management

resource sharing
UF: shared library resources
BT: cooperation
RT: interlibrary loans

response time
BT: (qualities of systems and
equipment)
RT: performance
search time

restoration
BT: preservation of library materials

retention of documents
BT: records management

retrieval effectiveness
BT: effectiveness
RT: evaluation
fallout
information retrieval
noise (information retrieval)
precision
recall
relevance

retrieval languages
USE: index languages

retrieval software
UF: search software
BT: computer software
RT: information retrieval
online searching

retrieval speed
USE: search time

retrospective cataloging
BT: cataloging (bibliographic)

retrospective conversion
SN: Of data to machine-readable
form.
BT: data conversion

reviewing
SN: Post-publication. For
pre-publication reviewing use
refereeing.
BT: evaluation

reviews
BT: (by information content, purpose)
NT: book reviews
literature reviews

reviews of the literature
USE: literature reviews

reviews, book
USE: book reviews

rewritable optical disks
   USE: erasable optical discs
RISC
   UF: reduced instruction set computers
   BT: computers
robotics
   SN: The study of machines that
           interact with their environment by
           moving around in it and/or
           manipulating it, in what could be
           considered an intelligent manner.
   BT: computer science
   NT: telerobotics
   RT: computer vision
           robots
robots
   BT: (hardware, equipment, and
           systems)
   RT: computer vision
           computers
           robotics
role indicators
   BT: (knowledge and information
           organization devices)
   RT: index languages
           links (between indexing terms)
           postcoordinate indexing
           subject indexing
rolling stacks
   USE: library shelving
ROM
   USE: read only memory
romanization
   BT: information processing
rotated indexes
   USE: permuted indexes
royalties
   BT: pricing
   RT: copyright
           public lending right
RT references
   USE: cross references
RT relationships
   USE: associative relationships
rule based systems
   USE: knowledge bases

sampling
   BT: statistical methods
satellite communications
   UF: communications satellites
   BT: telecommunications
satisfaction
   USE: user satisfaction
scanners
   UF: optical scanners
   BT: input equipment
   RT: scanning
scanning
   UF: optical scanning
   BT: data processing
   RT: optical recognition
           scanners
scatter (bibliometrics)
   BT: (qualities of information and
           data)
   RT: bibliometrics
           Bradford's law
scheduling
   BT: (business and management
           operations)
   RT: management
           planning
           strategic planning
scholarly journals
   USE: journals
scholarly publishing
   UF: academic publishing
   BT: publishing
   RT: journals
           monographs
school libraries
   USE: media centers
school media centers
   USE: media centers
scientific and technical information
   UF: STI
           technical information
   BT: information
   NT: chemical information
scientific societies
   USE: professional associations

scientometrics
  BT: infometrics
scope notes
  SN: Statements providing guidance to
         the usage or meaning of a term in
         a particular index language.
  UF: SN
  BT: syndetic structures
screen design
  BT: (computer operations)
         design
  RT: human computer interfaces
         video display terminals
scripts (writing systems)
  USE: writing systems
SDI services
  UF: selective dissemination of
         information
         user profiles
  BT: current awareness services
  RT: contents lists
         information dissemination
search behavior
  BT: user behavior
  RT: online searchers
         searching
search formulation
  USE: query formulation
search intermediaries
  USE: online searchers
search languages
  USE: index languages
search services
  SN: Organizations which sell, lease, or
         provide access to databases
         produced by other organizations.
  UF: database hosts
         database vendors
         host computers
         host services
  BT: vendors
  RT: database leasing
         database producers
         information industry

search services (cont.)
  RT: information infrastructure
         information utilities
         online industry
search software
  USE: retrieval software
search strategies
  BT: (knowledge and information
         organization devices)
  NT: hedges (online searching)
  RT: online searching
         searching
search systems
  USE: information retrieval systems
search term weighting
  USE: weighting
search terms
  BT: terms
  RT: index terms
         searching
         weighting
search time
  SN: Time expended by a user in
         searching; not system "response
         time."
  UF: retrieval speed
  BT: (qualities of systems and
         equipment)
  RT: performance
         response time
         searching
searchers
  USE: online searchers
searching
  BT: information retrieval
  NT: Boolean searching
         browsing
         citation searching
         end user searching
         exact match searching
         free text searching
         keyword searching
         known item searching
         natural language searching
         online searching
         proximity searching

searching (cont.)
- NT: query by example
  - query formulation
  - query refinement
  - range searching
  - sequential searching
  - string searching
  - subject searching
- RT: fuzzy retrieval systems
  - navigation
  - search behavior
  - search strategies
  - search terms
  - search time
  - truncation
  - weighting

Sears Subject Headings
- BT: subject heading lists

secondary information services
- USE: abstracting and indexing services

security
- BT: (business and management operations)
- NT: computer security
  - data security
- RT: privacy
  - security classification

security classification
- BT: (business and management operations)
- RT: confidential records
  - security

see also references
- USE: cross references

see references
- USE: cross references

selection (of materials)
- BT: collection development

selective dissemination of information
- USE: SDI services

semantic analysis
- BT: linguistic analysis

semantic networks
- SN: Graphic representations. For discussion of relationships in meaning, use semantic relationships.
- BT: networks
- RT: semantic relationships
  - semantics

semantic relationships
- BT: (linguistic elements)
- NT: antonymy
  - associative relationships
  - equivalence relationships
  - hierarchical relationships
  - homography
- RT: categories
  - semantic networks
  - semantics

semantics
- UF: meaning
- BT: semiotics
- RT: semantic networks
  - semantic relationships

semiotics
- BT: linguistics
- NT: pragmatics
  - semantics
  - syntactics

sensors
- BT: (hardware, equipment, and systems)
- RT: data collection
  - input equipment

sensory perception
- USE: perception (sensory)

sentence generation
- SN: Generation of natural language sentences from other representations.
- BT: natural language processing
- RT: sentences

sentences
- BT: (linguistic elements)
- RT: sentence generation

sequential searching
UF: serial searching
BT: searching

serendipity
BT: mental processes
RT: browsing

serial searching
USE: sequential searching

serials
BT: publications
NT: newspapers
periodicals
yearbooks
RT: standard serial numbers
subscriptions

series
BT: publications

service bureaus
BT: (product and service providers)

set theory
BT: mathematical methods
NT: fuzzy set theory
mapping (sets)
RT: fuzzy set theory
mathematics

shared cataloging
BT: cataloging (bibliographic)
cooperation

shared library resources
USE: resource sharing

shareware
BT: computer software

shelving
USE: storage (materials)

shelving, library
USE: library shelving

shopping, computer
USE: teleshopping

short term memory
UF: working memory
BT: memory (human)

sight
USE: vision

signal processing
BT: (computer operations)
RT: compression

signal processing (cont.)
RT: image processing
telecommunications

similarity
BT: (qualities of information and
data)
RT: feedback
relevance

simulation
BT: (research and analytic methods)
NT: computer simulation
RT: models

slides
BT: visual materials

small libraries
UF: one person libraries
solo librarians
BT: libraries

small presses
UF: underground presses
BT: publishers
RT: alternative publications

SN
USE: scope notes

social aspects
SN: Of information and information
use. For the discipline use social
sciences and its narrower terms.
UF: cultural aspects
BT: (sociocultural aspects)

social psychology
BT: psychology
social sciences

social sciences
BT: (fields and disciplines)
NT: anthropology
demographics
economics
education
law
political science
social psychology
socioeconomics
sociology
RT: area studies
behavioral sciences

societies
USE: professional associations

socioeconomics
BT: social sciences

sociograms
BT: graphics
RT: sociometrics

sociology
BT: behavioral sciences
social sciences
NT: organization theory
sociometrics

sociometrics
BT: sociology
RT: sociograms

software engineering
BT: computer programming
NT: computer aided software
engineering

software industry
UF: software publishers
BT: (product and service providers)
RT: computer industry
computer software
publishing

software publishers
USE: software industry

software, computer
USE: computer software

solo librarians
USE: small libraries

sort sequences
BT: (knowledge and information
organization devices)
RT: alphabetical arrangement
arrangement
sorting

sorting
BT: data processing
RT: sort sequences

sound
UF: acoustics
sounds
BT: (natural functions and events)
NT: noise (acoustic)

sound recordings
UF: audio recordings
audiodisk recordings
recordings, sound
BT: nonprint media
NT: audiotapes
talking books

sounds
USE: sound

special collections
BT: collections
RT: rare materials

special libraries
UF: clearinghouses (special libraries)
information centers (special
libraries)
BT: libraries
NT: corporate libraries
Presidential libraries

specificity (indexing)
BT: (qualities of information and
data)
RT: depth (indexing)
exhaustivity (indexing)
indexing
subject indexing

speech
BT: (natural functions and events)
RT: speech recognition
speech synthesis

speech production
USE: speech synthesis

speech recognition
UF: speech understanding
voice recognition
BT: natural language processing
RT: audio interfaces
speech

speech synthesis
SN: Mechanical generation of human
speech.
UF: speech production
synthesis, speech
voice synthesis
BT: natural language processing

speech synthesis (cont.)
RT: audio interfaces
speech
speech understanding
USE: speech recognition
spell checkers
USE: spelling checkers
spelling checkers
UF: spell checkers
BT: computer software
RT: typographical errors
word processing
spelling errors
USE: typographical errors
spreading activation
BT: (research and analytic methods)
RT: networks
ncural networks
spreadsheets
BT: (by information content, purpose)
RT: numeric data
SQL
USE: structured query languages
standard book numbers
UF: International Standard Book
Number
ISBN
BT: document surrogates
RT: books
standards
standard serial numbers
UF: International Standard Serial
Number
ISSN
BT: document surrogates
RT: serials
standards
standardization
BT: (general activities)
RT: benchmarks
evaluation
standards
standards
UF: guidelines
BT: (by information content, purpose)

standards (cont.)
RT: benchmarks
standard book numbers
standard serial numbers
standardization
standing orders
BT: ordering (materials)
state libraries
BT: government libraries
RT: state library agencies
state library agencies
BT: government agencies
RT: public libraries
state libraries
statistical databases
USE: numeric databases
statistical methods
BT: mathematical methods
NT: analysis of variance
Bayesian functions
Monte Carlo method
multivariate analysis
sampling
RT: factor analysis
mathematics
probability
statistical retrieval
USE: probabilistic retrieval
stemming
BT: truncation
RT: suffixes
STI
USE: scientific and technical
information
stochastic models
BT: mathematical models
RT: stochastic processes
stochastic processes
UF: random processes
BT: (natural functions and events)
NT: queuing
RT: cybernetics
probability
stochastic models
stop lists
USE: stoplists

stop words
USE: stoplists

stoplists
UF: stop lists
stop words
BT: (by information content, purpose)

storage (computer)
USE: computer storage

storage (materials)
UF: document storage
shelving
BT: (business and management
operations)
NT: compact storage
RT: library equipment
library shelving
moving
records management

storytelling
BT: communications
RT: children's services
library services

strategic planning
BT: planning
RT: forecasting
scheduling

string indexing
SN: Indexing methods which generate
a string or set of articulated index
terms for each entry.
BT: indexing

string searching
BT: searching
RT: proximity searching

structured query languages
UF: SQL
BT: query languages

students
BT: (persons and informal groups)
RT: education

subdivisions (indexing)
USE: modifiers

subheadings
USE: modifiers

subject access
BT: information access
RT: subject analysis
subject searching

subject analysis
UF: subject cataloguing
BT: organization of information
NT: subject indexing
vocabulary control
RT: subject access

subject cataloguing
USE: subject analysis

subject experts
UF: experts, subject
BT: (persons and informal groups)

subject heading lists
BT: controlled vocabularies
NT: Library of Congress Subject
Headings
Sears Subject Headings
RT: subject headings
thesauri

subject headings
BT: index terms
RT: descriptors
keywords
subject heading lists
vocabulary control

subject index terms
USE: index terms

subject indexes
BT: indexes (information retrieval)
RT: subject indexing
subject searching

subject indexing
BT: indexing
subject analysis
NT: chain indexing
generic posting
multilingual subject indexing
postcoordinate indexing
PRECIS
precoordinate indexing
RT: index languages
links (between indexing terms)
role indicators

subject indexing (cont.)
    RT: specificity (indexing)
          subject indexes
subject searching
    BT: searching
    RT: subject access
          subject indexes
subscription agencies
    BT: vendors
    RT: subscriptions
subscriptions
    BT: acquisitions (of materials)
    RT: claiming (acquisitions)
          serials
          subscription agencies
suffixes
    BT: (linguistic elements)
    RT: stemming
          syntactics
summaries
    USE: digests
summarization
    BT: text processing
    NT: abstracting
          extracting
supercomputers
    UF: high performance computing
    BT: computers
superimposed coding
    BT: encoding
superminicomputers
    BT: minicomputers
suppliers
    USE: vendors
support staff, library
    USE: paraprofessional library personnel
surnames
    USE: personal names
surrogates, document
    USE: document surrogates
surveillance
    USE: monitoring
surveys
    UF: questionnaires
    BT: (by information content, purpose)
    NT: library surveys

switching languages
    UF: intermediate index languages
          intermediate lexicons
    BT: controlled vocabularies
symbols
    BT: information representations
syndetic structures
    BT: controlled vocabularies
    NT: cross references
          scope notes
synonymous relationships
    USE: equivalence relationships
synonymy
    USE: equivalence relationships
syntactic analysis
    UF: parsing
    BT: linguistic analysis
    RT: syntactics
syntactics
    BT: semiotics
    RT: anaphora
          suffixes
          syntactic analysis
synthesis, notation
    USE: notation synthesis
synthesis, speech
    USE: speech synthesis
system knowledge
    BT: knowledge
systematic arrangement
    UF: classified arrangement
    BT: arrangement
    RT: classification
systems analysis
    BT: (research and analytic methods)
    RT: flow charting
          systems design
          systems development
systems design
    BT: (research and analytic methods)
    RT: flow charting
          modularity
          systems analysis
          systems development

systems development
- BT: (research and analytic methods)
- RT: systems analysis
  - systems design

systems integration
- UF: integration, systems
- BT: (business and management operations)

table of contents lists
- USE: contents lists

tactile sensations
- USE: perception (sensory)

talking books
- BT: books
  - sound recordings

tape leasing
- USE: database leasing

tape recorders
- BT: (hardware, equipment, and systems)
- NT: cassette recorders
  - video recorders

task knowledge
- BT: knowledge
- RT: domain knowledge

taxonomies
- USE: classification schemes

taxonomy
- SN: The study of natural classifications.
- BT: classification

taxonomy construction
- USE: index language construction

teaching
- USE: education

technical information
- USE: scientific and technical information

technical processes
- USE: technical services (libraries)

technical reports
- UF: reports, technical
- BT: grey literature
- RT: government publications
  - grey literature

technical services (libraries)
- UF: technical processes
- BT: library services
- NT: cataloging (bibliographic)
  - circulation (library)
  - collection development
  - interlibrary loans
- RT: binding
  - preservation of library materials

technical writing
- BT: authorship

technological gatekeepers
- USE: gatekeepers

technological innovation
- USE: innovation

technology impact
- BT: (sociocultural aspects)
- RT: innovation

technology transfer
- BT: (technical and manufacturing operations)
- RT: diffusion of innovation

telecommunications
- UF: telematics
- BT: communications
- NT: audio communications
  - broadcasting
  - computer mediated communications
  - data transmission
  - facsimile transmission
  - mobile communications
  - multiple access communications
  - multiplexing
  - packet switching
  - satellite communications
  - teleconferencing
  - telegraphy
  - teleshopping
  - teletext
  - traffic (network)
  - video communications
  - voice communications
- RT: communications protocols
  - information technology
  - signal processing

telecommunications (cont.)
RT: telecommunications equipment
telecommunications networks
transmission speed

telecommunications equipment
BT: (hardware, equipment, and systems)
NT: coaxial cable
fiber optics
modems
telephones
RT: telecommunications

telecommunications industry
UF: common carriers
BT: (product and service providers)
RT: information industry

telecommunications networks
UF: communications networks
computer networks
information networks
BT: networks
NT: common carrier networks
Internet
ISDN
local area networks
metropolitan area networks
National Research and Education Network
wide area networks
RT: library networks
telecommunications

telecommuting
BT: working at home

teleconferencing
BT: telecommunications
NT: video teleconferencing

telefacsimile
USE: facsimile transmission

telegraphy
BT: telecommunications

telemarketing
BT: marketing

telematics
USE: telecommunications

telemetry
BT: (research and analytic methods)
RT: remote sensing

telephones
BT: telecommunications equipment
NT: videotelephones
RT: voice transmission

telerobotics
BT: remote control
robotics

teleshopping
UF: shopping, computer
BT: telecommunications
RT: videotex

teletext
BT: telecommunications
RT: videotex

television
BT: mass media
video communications
NT: cable television
HDTV
pay per view television
RT: broadcasting

term frequency
USE: frequency of use

term weighting
USE: weighting

terminals, video display
USE: video display terminals

terminology
UF: definitions (of terms)
nomenclature
BT: information representations
NT: chemical nomenclature
RT: controlled vocabularies
dictionaries

terms
SN: Words or phrases used to denote concepts.
BT: information representations
NT: index terms
search terms
words
RT: words

testing
    BT: (research and analytic methods)
    NT: prototyping
    RT: experiments
           indexer consistency
           research and development
text analysis
    USE: text processing
text databases
    USE: full text databases
text editors
    BT: computer software
    RT: word processing
text processing
    UF: text analysis
    BT: information processing
    NT: content analysis
           editing
           linguistic analysis
           proofreading
           summarization
    RT: natural language processing
text retrieval
    USE: full text searching
textbases
    USE: full text databases
textbooks
    BT: books
textual databases
    USE: full text databases
theft detection systems
    USE: library security systems
thesauri
    BT: controlled vocabularies
    NT: graphical thesauri
           microthesauri
           multilingual thesauri
           thesaurus displays
    RT: candidate descriptors
           descriptors
           dictionaries
           index language construction
           index terms
           lexicography
           subject heading lists
           thesaurofacet

thesauri (cont.)
    RT: thesaurus maintenance
           vocabulary control
thesaurofacet
    SN: An indexing vocabulary which
           combines an alphabetical
           thesaurus and a faceted
           classification scheme.
    BT: controlled vocabularies
    RT: classification schemes
           faceted classification
           thesauri
thesaurus construction
    USE: index language construction
thesaurus displays
    UF: displays (thesauri)
    BT: thesauri
thesaurus maintenance
    UF: thesaurus updating
    BT: maintenance
    RT: index language construction
           thesauri
thesaurus updating
    USE: thesaurus maintenance
theses
    USE: dissertations
timeliness
    USE: currency (in time)
titles
    SN: Of documents.
    BT: (information representations)
    RT: KWIC indexes
           KWOC indexes
tomography
    BT: imaging
    RT: medical informatics
top terms
    SN: In thesauri, the name of the
           broadest class to which a specific
           concept belongs.
    UF: TT
    BT: index terms
touch screen interfaces
    UF: touch terminals
    BT: human computer interfaces
    RT: video display terminals

touch terminals
    USE: touch screen interfaces
trackballs (computer peripherals)
    BT: pointing devices
    RT: graphical user interfaces
          mice (computer peripherals)
trade secrets
    BT: (by content)
    RT: copyright
          intellectual property
trademarks
    BT: (information representations)
    RT: intellectual property
traffic (network)
    BT: telecommunications
training
    BT: (educational and psychological
          activities)
    NT: bibliographic instruction
          tutorials
          user training
    RT: education
transborder data flow
    UF: crossborder data flow
          international data flow
          transnational data flow
    BT: information flow
translation
    UF: interpretation (linguistic)
    BT: information processing
    NT: machine translation
translators
    UF: interpreters (linguistic)
    BT: information professionals
transliteration
    BT: information processing
transmission speed
    UF: baud rate
    BT: (qualities of systems and
          equipment)
    RT: modems
          telecommunications
transnational data flow
    USE: transborder data flow
transputers
    BT: computers

tree structures
    BT: data structures
truncation
    BT: information processing
    NT: stemming
    RT: searching
TT
    USE: top terms
turnkey systems
    BT: computer systems
tutorials
    BT: training
typesetting
    USE: typography
typographical errors
    UF: keyboarding errors
          misspellings
          spelling errors
    BT: errors
    RT: spelling checkers
typography
    UF: computer typesetting
          typesetting
    BT: (technical and manufacturing
          operations)
UDC
    USE: Universal Decimal Classification
UF references
    USE: cross references
UF relationships
    USE: equivalence relationships
uncertainty
    BT: (qualities of information and
          data)
    RT: ambiguity
          probability
uncontrolled indexing
    USE: keywords
underground presses
    USE: small presses
underground publications
    USE: alternative publications
understanding
    USE: comprehension
understanding (natural language)
    USE: natural language understanding

union catalogs
    BT: catalogs (bibliographic)
unions, labor
    USE: labor unions
Universal Decimal Classification
    UF: UDC
    BT: classification schemes
universities
    USE: colleges and universities
university libraries
    USE: academic libraries
up to dateness
    USE: currency (in time)
updating
    BT: maintenance
    RT: currency (in time)
uploading
    BT: file transfers
usability
    UF: ease of use
    BT: (general qualities)
    RT: accuracy
           complexity
           effectiveness
usage frequency
    USE: frequency of use
usage studies
    BT: user studies
use instruction
    USE: bibliographic instruction
use of information
    USE: information use
use references
    USE: cross references
use relationships
    USE: equivalence relationships
use studies
    USE: user studies
used for references
    USE: cross references
used for relationships
    USE: equivalence relationships
used terms
    USE: index terms

user aids
    BT: (by information content, purpose)
    RT: documentation
           help systems
           user training
           users
user behavior
    BT: human behavior
    NT: search behavior
    RT: user expectations
           user models
           user training
           users
user education
    USE: user training
user expectations
    BT: (natural functions and events)
    RT: user behavior
           user satisfaction
           users
user feedback
    USE: feedback
user information needs
    USE: information needs
user models
    SN: Models of users; for users' models
           of information or objects, use
           "cognitive models."
    BT: models
    RT: user behavior
           users
user needs
    USE: information needs
user profiles
    USE: SDI services
user satisfaction
    UF: satisfaction
    BT: (human qualities)
    RT: user expectations
           users
user studies
    UF: information user studies
           use studies
    BT: (research and analytic methods)
    NT: usage studies

user studies (cont.)
    RT: focus groups
           library surveys
           users
user system interfaces
    USE: human computer interfaces
user training
    UF: user education
    BT: training
    RT: bibliographic instruction
           information literacy
           user aids
           user behavior
           users
users
    UF: information users
           library patrons
           patrons
    BT: (persons and informal groups)
    NT: end users
           library users
    RT: bibliographic instruction
           information needs
           information use
           user aids
           user behavior
           user expectations
           user models
           user satisfaction
           user studies
           user training
utility
    BT: (general qualities)
utility software
    BT: computer software
validation
    BT: data processing
    RT: error correction
           error detection
           error messages
           error rates
           errors
           verification

value added
    BT: (general qualities)
    RT: abstracting and indexing services
           databases
           information services
value of information
    USE: economics of information
VCR
    USE: videocassette recorders
VDT
    USE: video display terminals
VDU
    USE: video display terminals
vector analysis
    BT: mathematical methods
    RT: vector space models
vector space models
    BT: models
    RT: vector analysis
vendors
    SN: Very broad term; prefer specific
           product or service, e.g., "book
           vendors;" "consulting services."
    UF: suppliers
    BT: (product and service providers)
    NT: book vendors
           search services
           subscription agencies
verification
    BT: data processing
    RT: error correction
           error detection
           error rates
           errors
           validation
vertical files
    BT: (by medium, physical form)
very large scale integration
    USE: VLSI
video communications
    BT: telecommunications
    NT: television
           video teleconferencing
video conferencing
    USE: video teleconferencing

video display terminals
- UF: cathode ray tube terminals
  CRT terminals
  graphics terminals
  terminals, video display
  VDT
  VDU
  visual display terminals
- BT: computer peripherals
  displays
- RT: input equipment
  output equipment
  screen design
  touch screen interfaces

video games
- UF: computer games
- BT: computer software
- RT: joysticks

video materials
- USE: video recordings

video recorders
- BT: tape recorders
- NT: videocassette recorders

video recordings
- UF: video materials
- BT: visual materials
- NT: motion video
  videocassettes

video teleconferencing
- UF: video conferencing
- BT: teleconferencing
  video communications

videocassette recorders
- UF: VCR
- BT: cassette recorders
  video recorders
- RT: videocassettes

videocassettes
- BT: video recordings
- RT: videocassette recorders

videodiscs
- UF: videodisks
- BT: optical discs

videodisks
- USE: videodiscs

videophones
- USE: videotelephones

videotelephones
- UF: picture telephones
  videophones
- BT: telephones

videotex
- BT: (communications media)
- RT: teleshopping
  teletext

virtual libraries
- SN: Systems in which information resources are distributed via networks, rather than being physically held in a particular location.
- BT: libraries
- RT: cooperation
  document delivery
  library automation

virtual memory
- BT: memory (computer)

virtual reality
- BT: computer software

viruses (computer)
- UF: computer viruses
- BT: computer software
- RT: computer crime

vision
- UF: sight
- BT: (natural functions and events)
- NT: computer vision

visual display terminals
- USE: video display terminals

visual information
- USE: visual materials

visual materials
- UF: visual information
  visual resources
- BT: nonprint media
- NT: films
  filmstrips
  images
  realia
  slides
  video recordings

visual materials (cont.)
- RT: art
  films
  filmstrips
  maps

visual memory
- BT: memory (human)
- RT: visualization

visual resources
- USE: visual materials

visualization
- BT: mental processes
- RT: visual memory

VLSI
- UF: very large scale integration
- BT: LSI

vocabulary control
- BT: subject analysis
- RT: assignment indexing
  controlled vocabularies
  index language construction
  literary warrant
  subject headings
  thesauri

voice communications
- BT: telecommunications
- NT: voice mail

voice input
- USE: audio interfaces

voice mail
- BT: message systems
  voice communications

voice recognition
- USE: speech recognition

voice synthesis
- USE: speech synthesis

voice transmission
- BT: data transmission
- RT: telephones

volunteers
- BT: (persons and informal groups)

WAN
- USE: wide area networks

weeding
- USE: deselection

weighting
- UF: index term weighting
  query weighting
  search term weighting
  term weighting
- BT: information processing
- RT: index terms
  indexing
  search terms
  searching

what you see is what you get
- USE: WYSIWYG

wide area networks
- UF: WAN
- BT: telecommunications networks

windows interfaces
- USE: graphical user interfaces

wire services
- USE: newswire services

word by word arrangement
- UF: nothing before something arrangement
- BT: alphabetical arrangement

word co-occurrence analysis
- USE: co-occurrence analysis

word frequency
- BT: frequency of use
- RT: Zipf's law

word processing
- BT: data processing
- RT: spelling checkers
  text editors

word recognition
- BT: pattern recognition
- RT: words

words
- BT: terms
- RT: etymology
  lexicography
  terms
  word recognition

work flow analysis
- BT: (research and analytic methods)

working at home
    UF: home work
    BT: employment
    NT: telecommuting
working memory
    USE: short term memory
workshops
    BT: meetings
    RT: continuing education
         meetings
workstations
    BT: computers
world knowledge
    USE: common sense knowledge
WORM discs
    UF: write once read many
    BT: optical discs
    NT: DRAW
write once read many
    USE: WORM discs
writers
    USE: authors
writing
    USE: authorship

writing systems
    UF: scripts (writing systems)
    BT: information representations
    NT: alphabets
         Braille
         ideographs
         nonroman scripts
WYSIWYG
    UF: what you see is what you get
    BT: (qualities of systems and
         equipment)
    RT: desktop publishing
         graphical user interfaces
         graphics
yearbooks
    BT: reference materials
         serials
young adult literature
    UF: adolescent literature
    BT: (by information content, purpose)
    RT: young adult services
young adult services
    BT: library services
    RT: young adult literature
Zipf's law
    BT: infometrics
    RT: word frequency

Hierarchical Display

(activities and operations)
. (business and management operations)
. . accounting
. . . auditing
. . business
. . centralization
. . cooperation
. . . resource sharing
. . . shared cataloging*
. . decentralization
. . group work
. . management
. . . computing resource management
. . . critical incident method
. . . critical path method
. . . financial management
. . . . budgeting
. . . . cost recovery
. . . . grants
. . . human resource management
. . . information resources management
. . . . collection management
. . . . . collection assessment
. . . . . collection development
. . . . . . acquisitions (of materials)
. . . . approval plans
. . . . claiming (acquisitions)
. . . . gifts and exchanges
. . . . ordering (materials)
. . . . blanket orders
. . . . standing orders
. . . . subscriptions
. . . . . . deselection
. . . . . . selection (of materials)
. . . . records management
. . . . . retention of documents
. . . inventory
. . . library management
. . marketing
. . . advertising
. . . promotion
. . . . library weeks
. . . telemarketing
. . moving

(activities and operations) (cont.)
. (business and management operations)
(cont.)
. . planning
. . . strategic planning
. . pricing
. . . fees for service
. . . royalties
. . scheduling
. . security
. . . computer security
. . . . access control (computer systems)
. . . data security
. . security classification
. . storage (materials)
. . . compact storage
. . systems integration
. (communications activities)
. . communications
. . . authorship
. . . . technical writing
. . . communications patterns
. . . communications skills
. . . disclosure
. . . electronic communications
. . . . error messages
. . . explanation
. . . face to face communications
. . . . meetings
. . . . . workshops
. . . . nonverbal communications
. . . feedback
. . . informal communications
. . . negotiation
. . . oral communications
. . . . presearch interviews
. . . . reference interviews
. . . organizational communications
. . . personal networking
. . . public relations
. . . publishing
. . . . desktop publishing
. . . . electronic publishing
. . . . micropublishing
. . . . scholarly publishing

(activities and operations) (cont.)
. (communications activities) (cont.)
.. communications (cont.)
... reading
... storytelling
... telecommunications
.... audio communications
.... broadcasting
.... computer mediated communications
..... computer conferencing
..... message systems
...... bulletin board systems
...... electronic mail
...... listservs
...... voice mail
.... data transmission
.... broadband transmission
..... communications protocols
..... digital communications
..... electronic data interchange
..... electronic filing
..... file transfers
...... downloading
...... uploading
..... voice transmission
.... facsimile transmission
.... mobile communications
..... cellular communications
.... multiple access communications
.... multiplexing
.... packet switching
.... satellite communications
.... teleconferencing
..... video teleconferencing
.... telegraphy
.... teleshopping
.... teletext
.... traffic (network)
.... video communications
..... television
...... cable television
...... HDTV
...... pay per view television
..... video teleconferencing*
.... voice communications
..... voice mail*

(activities and operations) (cont.)
. (computer operations)
.. animation
.. authoring (hypermedia)
.. automatic...
.. automation
... library automation
.... computerized cataloging*
... office automation
.. computer aided design*
.. computer aided engineering*
.. computer aided manufacturing*
.. computer applications
.. computer integrated manufacturing*
.. computer programming
... logic programming
... object oriented programming
... software engineering
.... computer aided software engineering
.. data processing
... batch processing
... compression
... cross matching
... cryptography
.... decryption
.... encryption
... data conversion
.... database conversion
.... digital to analog conversion
.... digitization
.... retrospective conversion
... data distribution
... data entry
... data reduction
... decoding
... encoding
.... hash coding
.... superimposed coding
... end user computing
... form filling
... formatting
... multiprocessing
... multitasking
... normalization
... parallel processing
... pattern recognition
.... object recognition

(activities and operations) (cont.)
. (computer operations) (cont.)
. . data processing (cont.)
. . . pattern recognition (cont.)
. . . . optical recognition
. . . . . optical character recognition
. . . . . . feature extraction
. . . . . . font learning
. . . . word recognition
. . . real time processing
. . . scanning
. . . sorting
. . . validation
. . . verification
. . . word processing
. . distributed computing
. . documentation*
. . electronic funds transfer systems
. . flow charting
. . holography
. . imaging
. . . magnetic resonance imaging
. . . tomography
. . information processing
. . . graph processing
. . . image processing
. . . . image analysis
. . . . image enhancement
. . . query processing
. . . romanization
. . . text processing
. . . . content analysis
. . . . editing
. . . . linguistic analysis
. . . . . disambiguation
. . . . . lexical analysis
. . . . . morphological analysis
. . . . . semantic analysis
. . . . . syntactic analysis
. . . . proofreading
. . . . summarization
. . . . . abstracting
. . . . . . automatic abstracting
. . . . . extracting
. . . . . . automatic extracting
. . . translation
. . . . machine translation

(activities and operations) (cont.)
. (computer operations) (cont.)
. . information processing (cont.)
. . . transliteration
. . . truncation
. . . . stemming
. . . weighting
. . online computing
. . . online searching*
. . online...
. . pen based computing
. . screen design*
. . signal processing
. (educational and psychological activities)
. . accreditation
. . bibliotherapy
. . learning
. . . lifelong learning
. . . machine learning
. . . . font learning*
. . . perceptual learning
. . training
. . . bibliographic instruction
. . . tutorials
. . . user training
. (general activities)
. . design
. . . computer aided design
. . . database design
. . . forms design
. . . screen design
. . evaluation
. . . benchmarks
. . . refereeing
. . . reviewing
. . identification
. . maintenance
. . . database maintenance
. . . thesaurus maintenance
. . . updating
. . monitoring
. . standardization
. (information and library operations)
. . access to resources
. . . bibliographic access
. . . document access

(activities and operations) (cont.)
. (information and library operations)
(cont.)
.. access to resources (cont.)
... information access
.... subject access
... library access
... remote access
.. arrangement
... alphabetical arrangement
.... letter by letter arrangement
.... word by word arrangement
... systematic arrangement
.. bibliographic control
.. bibliography
... analytical bibliography
.. book collecting
.. database leasing
.. document delivery
... facsimile transmission*
... interlibrary loans*
.. document handling
.. document retrieval
.. documentation
.. genealogy
.. information dissemination
.. information flow
... information filtering
... transborder data flow
.. information production
.. information resources management*
.. information retrieval
... answer passage retrieval
... associative retrieval
... image retrieval
... probabilistic retrieval
... searching
.... Boolean searching
.... browsing
.... citation searching
.... end user searching
.... exact match searching
.... free text searching
..... full text searching
.... keyword searching
.... known item searching
.... natural language searching

(activities and operations) (cont.)
. (information and library operations)
(cont.)
.. information retrieval (cont.)
... searching (cont.)
.... online searching
..... crossfile searching
.... proximity searching
.... query by example
.... query formulation
.... query refinement
..... query expansion
.... range searching
.... sequential searching
.... string searching
.... subject searching
.. information seeking
.. information services
... community information services
... current awareness services
.... SDI services
... home information services
... litigation support
.. information transfer
.. information use
.. knowledge engineering
... knowledge acquisition
... knowledge representation
.. library services
... children's services
... library programs
... off campus library services
... outreach services (library)
... reader services
... reference services
.... reference interviews*
... technical services (libraries)
.... cataloging (bibliographic)*
.... circulation (library)
.... collection development*
.... interlibrary loans
... young adult services
.. navigation
.. organization of information
... cataloging (bibliographic)
.... cataloging in publication
.... computerized cataloging

(activities and operations) (cont.)
. (information and library operations)
            (cont.)
. . organization of information (cont.)
. . . cataloging (bibliographic) (cont.)
. . . . descriptive cataloging
. . . . minimal cataloging
. . . . retrospective cataloging
. . . . shared cataloging
. . . classification
. . . . automatic classification
. . . . faceted classification
. . . . hierarchical classification
. . . . notation synthesis
. . . . taxonomy
. . . database design*
. . . facet analysis
. . . index language construction
. . . indexing
. . . . assignment indexing
. . . . automatic indexing
. . . . book indexing
. . . . database indexing
. . . . derivative indexing
. . . . manual indexing
. . . . name indexing
. . . . periodical indexing
. . . . probabilistic indexing
. . . . string indexing
. . . . subject indexing
. . . . . chain indexing
. . . . . generic posting
. . . . . multilingual subject indexing
. . . . . postcoordinate indexing
. . . . . PRECIS
. . . . . precoordinate indexing
. . . relevance ranking
. . . subject analysis
. . . . subject indexing*
. . . . vocabulary control
. . output reformatting
. . photocopying
. . preservation of library materials
. . . binding
. . . conservation of library materials
. . . restoration
. . relevance judgments

(activities and operations) (cont.)
. (socioeconomic activities)
. . competition
. . computer crime
. . diffusion of innovation
. . employment
. . . working at home
. . . . telecommuting
. . entrepreneurship
. . innovation
. (technical and manufacturing operations)
. . computer aided engineering
. . computer aided manufacturing
. . computer integrated manufacturing
. . flexible manufacturing systems
. . printing
. . quality assurance
. . quality control
. . . duplicate detection
. . . error correction
. . . error detection
. . recording
. . . magnetic recording
. . . optical recording
. . technology transfer
. . typography
(buildings and facilities)
. buildings
. . library buildings
. computer centers
. computer laboratories
(communications media)
. audiotex
. mass media
. . newspapers*
. . radio
. . television*
. videotex
(document types)
. (by availability, access, organization)
. . banned materials
. . collections
. . . library collections
. . . personal collections
. . . special collections
. . foreign language materials

(document types) (cont.)
. (by availability, access, organization)
                 (cont.)
. . grey literature
. . . preprints
. . . technical reports
. . publications
. . . alternative publications
. . . books
. . . . paperbacks
. . . . talking books
. . . . textbooks
. . . electronic publications
. . . . electronic journals
. . government publications
. . monographs
. . out of print publications
. . print materials
. . . large print materials
. . serials
. . . . newspapers
. . . periodicals
. . . . . journals
. . . . . . electronic journals*
. . . . . newsletters
. . . . periodical articles
. . . yearbooks
. . series
. rare materials
. (by information content, purpose)
. . bibliographies
. . . national bibliographies
. . catalogs (bibliographic)
. . . card catalogs
. . . classified catalogs
. . . OPACs
. . . union catalogs
. . children's literature
. . core literature
. . correspondence
. . data
. . . analog data
. . . machine readable data
. . . numeric data
. . personal data

(document types) (cont.)
. (by information content, purpose) (cont.)
. . databases
. . . bibliographic databases
. . . . full text databases
. . . . OPACs*
. . . data dictionaries
. . . deductive databases
. . . distributed databases
. . . nonbibliographic databases
. . . . community resource files
. . . . fact databases
. . . . . numeric databases
. . . . human resource files
. . . . image databases
. . . object oriented databases
. . . online databases
. . . . OPACs*
. . . relational databases
. . dissertations
. . document surrogates
. . . abstracts
. . . . author abstracts
. . . annotations
. . . bibliographic records
. . . . bibliographic citations
. . . . MARC records
. . . contents lists
. . . digests
. . . standard book numbers
. . . standard serial numbers
. . ephemera
. . erotic materials
. . files
. . . authority files
. . . inverted files
. . . personal files
. . indexes (information retrieval)
. . . alphabetico classed indexes
. . . author indexes
. . . author-prepared indexes
. . . book indexes
. . . citation indexes
. . . cumulative indexes
. . . keyword indexes
. . . . concordances
. . . . KWIC indexes

(document types) (cont.)
. (by information content, purpose) (cont.)
.. indexes (information retrieval) (cont.)
... keyword indexes (cont.)
.... KWOC indexes
.... permuted indexes
... periodical indexes
... subject indexes
.. information sources
... human information sources
.. library materials
... overdue materials
.. marginalia
.. patents
.. popular materials
.. pornographic materials
.. primary literature
.. records
... administrative records
... bibliographic records*
... confidential records
... duplicate records
... medical records
... public records
.. reference materials
... almanacs
... dictionaries
... directories
... encyclopedias
... handbooks
... loose leaf services
... ready reference materials
... yearbooks*
.. reviews
... book reviews
... literature reviews
.. spreadsheets
.. standards
.. stoplists
.. surveys
... library surveys
.. user aids
.. young adult literature
. (by medium, physical form)
.. books*

(document types) (cont.)
. (by medium, physical form) (cont.)
.. computer software
... artificial intelligence
.... computer vision
.... expert systems
.... machine learning*
.... natural language processing
..... discourse analysis
..... discourse generation
..... natural language understanding
..... sentence generation
..... speech recognition
..... speech synthesis
.... neural networks*
... courseware
... database management systems
... decision support systems
.... group decision support systems
... groupware
... information retrieval systems
.... executive information systems
.... fact retrieval systems
.... fuzzy retrieval systems
.... geographic information systems
.... image information systems
.... management information systems
.... paper based information systems
.... reference retrieval systems
... microprograms
... operating systems
... public domain software
... retrieval software
... shareware
... spelling checkers
... text editors
... utility software
... video games
... virtual reality
... viruses (computer)
.. electronic publications*
.. engineering drawings
.. graphics
... computer graphics
... sociograms
.. hypermedia
.. hypertext

(document types) (cont.)
. (by medium, physical form) (cont.)
.. illustrations
.. knowledge bases
.. manuscripts
.. maps
.. media
.. multimedia
.. nonprint media
... sound recordings
.... audiotapes*
.... talking books*
... visual materials
.... films
.... filmstrips
.... images
..... bit-mapped images
..... digitized images
..... photographs
.... realia
.... slides
.... video recordings
..... motion video
..... videocassettes
.. organization charts
.. physical objects
.. vertical files
(fields and disciplines)
. aerospace
. architecture
. area studies
. behavioral sciences
.. anthropology
.. psychology
... psychometrics
... social psychology
.. sociology*
. cartography
. cognitive science
. computer science
.. dynamic systems
.. robotics
... telerobotics
. cybernetics
. decision theory
. engineering
. finance

(fields and disciplines) (cont.)
. fine arts
.. art
.. music
. human factors
.. ergonomics
. humanities
.. history
.. lexicography
... computational lexicography
.. linguistics
... computational linguistics
... etymology
... grammars
.... case grammar
.. phonetics
.. semiotics
... pragmatics
... semantics
... syntactics
.. literature*
.. logic
... Boolean logic
... predicate logic
... propositional logic
.. philosophy
. informatics
.. medical informatics
.. museum informatics
. information science
.. economics of information*
.. information theory
. librarianship
.. comparative librarianship
.. international librarianship
. mathematics
.. operations research
. natural sciences
.. biomedical sciences
... biology
... medicine
... pharmacology
.. earth sciences
.. ecology
.. geography
. performing arts

(fields and disciplines) (cont.)
. physical sciences
.. chemistry
.. physics
. social sciences
.. anthropology*
.. demographics
.. economics
... econometrics
... economics of information
.. education
... adult education
... basic education
... computer assisted instruction
... continuing education
... distance learning
.... correspondence study
... home education
... information science education
... library education
... off campus education
.. law
.. political science
.. social psychology*
.. socioeconomics
.. sociology
... organization theory
... sociometrics
(hardware, equipment, and systems)
. cameras
. computer systems
.. analog systems
.. client server systems
.. dedicated systems
.. human computer interfaces
... audio interfaces
... command driven interfaces
... error messages*
... front ends
... gateways
... graphical user interfaces
... help systems
... intelligent interfaces
.... natural language interfaces
... menu based interfaces
... touch screen interfaces
.. hybrid systems

(hardware, equipment, and systems) (cont.)
. computer systems (cont.)
.. hypercube systems
.. interactive systems
.. turnkey systems
. control systems
.. remote control
... telerobotics*
. displays
.. color displays
.. high resolution displays
.. video display terminals*
. educational technology
. information technology
.. computer equipment
... computer peripherals
.... computer storage
..... archival storage
..... disk drives
...... CD-ROM drives
.... jukeboxes
..... high density storage
.... input equipment
..... joysticks
..... keyboards
..... light pens
..... pointing devices
...... mice (computer peripherals)
...... trackballs (computer peripherals)
..... scanners
.... output equipment
..... printers (equipment)
.... video display terminals
... computers
.... computer architectures
.... database machines
.... file servers
..... image servers
.... mainframe computers
.... memory (computer)
..... associative memory
..... content addressable memory
..... holographic memory
..... random access memory
...... DRAM
..... read only memory
..... virtual memory

(hardware, equipment, and systems) (cont.)
. information technology (cont.)
.. computer equipment (cont.)
... computers (cont.)
.... microcomputers
..... personal computers
.... minicomputers
..... superminicomputers
.... optical computers
.... optoelectronic computers
.... processing units (computers)
..... array processors
..... back end processors
..... microprocessors
..... multiprocessors
..... parallel processors
.... RISC
.... supercomputers
.... transputers
.... workstations
... integrated circuits
.... LSI
..... VLSI
. instrumentation
. integrated systems
.. integrated library systems
. lasers
. library equipment
.. library security systems
.. library shelving
. library supplies
. optical equipment
.. optical computers*
.. optical media*
. photocopiers
. robots
. sensors
. tape recorders
.. cassette recorders
... videocassette recorders
.. video recorders
... videocassette recorders*
. telecommunications equipment
.. coaxial cable
.. fiber optics
.. modems

(hardware, equipment, and systems) (cont.)
. telecommunications equipment (cont.)
.. telephones
... videotelephones
(knowledge, information, etc.)
. (by content)
.. algorithms
.. competitive intelligence
.. default values
.. errors
... typographical errors
.. genomes
.. indicators (values)
.. information
... company information
... consumer information
... public information
... scientific and technical information
.... chemical information
..... chemical nomenclature
..... chemical structures
..... connection tables (chemistry)
.. knowledge
... common sense knowledge
... concepts
... domain knowledge
... system knowledge
... task knowledge
.. literature
... fiction
... poetry
.. music*
.. news
.. nonfiction
.. oral history
.. proper names
... corporate names
... personal names
.. trade secrets
. (information representations)
.. information representations
... abbreviations
... acronyms
... anaphora
... bar codes
... character sets
... chemical structures*

(knowledge, information, etc.) (cont.)
. (information representations) (cont.)
. . information representations (cont.)
. . . connection tables (chemistry)*
. . . diacriticals
. . . graphs
. . . icons
. . . idioms
. . . metaphors
. . . . desktop metaphor
. . . notation
. . . symbols
. . . terminology
. . . . chemical nomenclature*
. . . terms
. . . . index terms
. . . . . candidate descriptors
. . . . . descriptors
. . . . . identifiers
. . . . . keywords
. . . . . modifiers
. . . . . qualifiers
. . . . . subject headings
. . . . . top terms
. . . . search terms
. . . . words
. . . writing systems
. . . . alphabets
. . . . Braille
. . . . ideographs
. . . . nonroman scripts
. . titles
. . trademarks
. (knowledge and information organization
                    devices)
. . access points
. . . entries
. . . entry vocabularies
. . . headings
. . . links (hypertext)
. . cataloging rules
. . . Anglo American Cataloguing Rules
. . categories
. . data formats
. . . interchange formats
. . . . MARC formats

(knowledge, information, etc.) (cont.)
. (knowledge and information organization
                    devices) (cont.)
. . data structures
. . . abstract data types
. . . . objects (data structures)
. . . tree structures
. . file structures
. . . hierarchical file structures
. . hierarchies
. . links (between indexing terms)
. . locators
. . mapping (graphic representation)
. . matrices
. . paradigms
. . role indicators
. . search strategies
. . . hedges (online searching)
. . sort sequences
. (languages)
. . languages
. . . command languages
. . . . common command language
. . . context free languages
. . . English language
. . . foreign languages
. . . index languages
. . . . classification schemes
. . . . . Dewey Decimal Classification
. . . . . International Patent Classification
. . . . . Library of Congress Classification
. . . . . Universal Decimal Classification
. . . . controlled vocabularies
. . . . . subject heading lists
. . . . . . Library of Congress Subject
                        Headings
. . . . . . Sears Subject Headings
. . . . switching languages
. . . . syndetic structures
. . . . . cross references
. . . . . scope notes
. . . . thesauri
. . . . . graphical thesauri
. . . . . microthesauri
. . . . . multilingual thesauri
. . . . . thesaurus displays
. . . . thesaurofacet

(knowledge, information, etc.) (cont.)
. (languages) (cont.)
. . languages (cont.)
. . . index languages (cont.)
. . . . documentary languages
. . . jargon
. . . markup languages
. . . programming languages
. . . . high level languages
. . . query languages
. . . . structured query languages
. (linguistic elements)
. . phrases
. . semantic relationships
. . . antonymy
. . . associative relationships
. . . equivalence relationships
. . . . quasi-synonymous relationships
. . . hierarchical relationships
. . . . genus species relationships
. . . . part whole relationships
. . . homography
. . sentences
. . suffixes
(natural functions and events)
. aging of materials
. data corruption
. disasters
. entropy (information)
. growth
. information explosion
. information life cycle
. memory (human)
. . long term memory
. . short term memory
. . visual memory
. mental processes
. . abstraction
. . cognition
. . comprehension
. . generalization
. . perception (conceptual)
. . perception (sensory)
. . reasoning
. . . inference
. . serendipity
. . visualization

(natural functions and events) (cont.)
. radiation
. sound
. . noise (acoustic)
. speech
. stochastic processes
. . queuing
. user expectations
. vision
. . computer vision*
(networks)
. networks
. . library networks
. . neural networks
. . nodes
. . semantic networks
. telecommunications networks
. . . common carrier networks
. . . Internet
. . . ISDN
. . . local area networks
. . . metropolitan area networks
. . . National Research and Education
Network
. . . wide area networks
(organizations)
. organizations
. . armed forces
. . consortia
. . friends of libraries
. . labor unions
. . professional associations
. . . information associations
. . . library associations
(persons and informal groups)
. authors
. . coauthors
. disabled persons
. . learning disabled persons
. . reading disabled persons
. early adopters
. employees
. entrepreneurs
. focus groups
. gatekeepers
. human information sources*

(persons and informal groups) (cont.)
. information workers
. . information professionals
. . . archivists
. . . editors
. . . information scientists
. . . librarians
. . . . reference librarians
. . . media specialists
. . . online searchers
. . . records managers
. . . translators
. . library personnel
. . . librarians*
. . . paraprofessional library personnel
. managers
. physicians
. students
. subject experts
. users
. . end users
. . . novice users
. . library users
. . . problem patrons
. volunteers
(physical media)
. disks
. . magnetic disks
. . . floppy disks
. . . hard disks
. . . magneto-optical disks
. . optical discs*
. magnetic media
. . magnetic disks*
. . magnetic tapes
. . . audiotapes
. . . . audiocassettes
. . . . digital audio tapes
. microforms
. . computer output microform
. . microfiche
. . microfilm
. optical media
. . optical discs
. . . compact discs
. . . . CD-ROM
. . . . compact disc interactive

(physical media) (cont.)
. optical media (cont.)
. . optical discs (cont.)
. . . compact discs (cont.)
. . . . digital video interactive
. . . erasable optical discs
. . . floptical discs
. . . magneto-optical disks*
. . . videodiscs
. . . WORM discs
. . . . DRAW
. . optical tape
. paper
. photographic films
(product and service providers)
. archives
. bibliographic utilities
. binderies
. colleges and universities
. . academic libraries*
. . library schools
. computer industry
. consultants
. government agencies
. . state library agencies
. information analysis centers
. information brokers
. information industry
. . online industry
. information infrastructure
. information utilities
. libraries
. . academic libraries
. . . community college libraries
. . branch libraries
. . central libraries
. . children's libraries
. . depository libraries
. . government libraries
. . . state libraries
. . institutional libraries
. . media centers
. . mobile libraries
. . . bookmobiles
. . national libraries
. . public libraries

(product and service providers) (cont.)
. libraries (cont.)
. . research libraries
. . . Presidential libraries
. . small libraries
. . special libraries
. . . corporate libraries
. . . Presidential libraries*
. . virtual libraries
. library suppliers
. museums
. publishers
. . database producers
. . . abstracting and indexing services
. . newswire services
. . small presses
. service bureaus
. software industry
. telecommunications industry
. vendors
. . book vendors
. . search services
. . subscription agencies
(qualities)
. (general qualities)
. . accuracy
. . compatibility
. . complexity
. . costs
. . . overhead costs
. . durability
. . effectiveness
. . . cost effectiveness
. . . retrieval effectiveness
. . efficiency
. . obsolescence
. . performance
. . permanence
. . physical location
. . probability
. . quality
. . reliability
. . usability
. . utility
. . value added
. (human qualities)
. . cognitive styles

(qualities) (cont.)
. (human qualities) (cont.)
. . creativity
. . indexer consistency
. . information needs
. . library skills
. . . reference skills
. . logical skills
. . productivity
. . user satisfaction
. (qualities of information and data)
. . aboutness
. . aging of literatures
. . ambiguity
. . citation order
. . currency (in time)
. . depth (indexing)
. . error rates
. . exhaustivity (indexing)
. . fallout
. . file integrity
. . frequency of use
. . . word frequency
. . intellectual property
. . . copyright
. . . public lending right
. . interdisciplinarity
. . legibility
. . literary warrant
. . noise (information retrieval)
. . overlap
. . precision
. . recall
. . relevance
. . scatter (bibliometrics)
. . similarity
. . specificity (indexing)
. . uncertainty
. (qualities of systems and equipment)
. . connectivity
. . fault tolerance
. . look and feel
. . maintainability
. . modularity
. . response time
. . search time
. . transmission speed

(qualities) (cont.)
. (qualities of systems and equipment)
                              (cont.)
. . WYSIWYG
(research and analytic methods)
. automata
. case studies
. cluster analysis
. co-occurrence analysis
. cost benefit analysis
. data analysis
. data collection
. decision making
. experiments
. forecasting
. mathematical methods
. . factor analysis
. . finitc element analysis
. . Fourier analysis
. . game theory
. . graph theory
. . Hough transformation
. . linear programming
. . nonlinear programming
. . set theory
. . . fuzzy set theory
. . . mapping (sets)
. . statistical methods
. . . analysis of variance
. . . Bayesian functions
. . . Monte Carlo method
. . . multivariate analysis
. . . sampling
. . vector analysis
. measurement
. . econometrics*
. . infometrics
. . . bibliometrics
. . . . Bradford's law
. . . . citation analysis
. . . . . bibliographic coupling
. . . . . cocitation analysis
. . . . Lotka's law
. . . scientometrics
. . . Zipf's law
. . photogrammetry
. . psychometrics*

(research and analytic methods) (cont.)
. models
. . connectionist models
. . database models
. . . relational models
. . hierarchical models
. . information models
. . . cognitive models
. . . data models
. . mathematical models
. . . Markov models
. . . stochastic models
. . predictive models
. . user models
. . vector space models
. needs assessment
. network analysis
. optimization
. problem solving
. . heuristics
. . participative problem solving
. remote sensing
. research and development
. . empirical studies
. . mission oriented research
. . qualitative research
. . research methods
. simulation
. . computer simulation
. spreading activation
. systems analysis
. systems design
. systems development
. telemetry
. testing
. . prototyping
. user studies
. . usage studies
. work flow analysis
(sectors of the economy)
. information sector (economy)
. private sector
. public sector
(sociocultural aspects)
. bilingualism
. censorship
. change

(sociocultural aspects) (cont.)
. civil rights
. . academic freedom
. . intellectual freedom
. . . freedom of information
. . . freedom to read
. . privacy
. computer literacy
. ethics
. gender
. goals
. human behavior
. . user behavior
. . . search behavior
. individual differences
. information literacy
. information overload
. information society
. language barriers

(sociocultural aspects) (cont.)
. legal aspects
. . admissibility of records
. . legal deposit
. . liability
. literacy
. organizational culture
. organizational environment
. politics
. psychological aspects
. . attitudes
. . intelligence
. . leadership
. . motivation
. public policy
. . information policy
. social aspects
. technology impact

Rotated Display

```
                    abbreviations
                    aboutness
                    abstract data types
                    abstracting
                    abstracting and indexing services
          automatic abstracting
                    abstraction
                    abstracts
             author abstracts
                    academic freedom
                    academic libraries
                    access control (computer systems)
                    access points
                    access to resources
      bibliographic access
           document access
        information access
            library access
             remote access
            subject access
           multiple access communications
            random access memory
                    accounting
                    accreditation
                    accuracy
              noise (acoustic)
          knowledge acquisition
                    acquisitions (of materials)
           claiming (acquisitions)
                    acronyms
          spreading activation
              value added
            content addressable memory
                    administrative records
                    admissibility of records
              early adopters
                    adult education
              young adult literature
              young adult services
                    advertising
                    aerospace
         government agencies
      state library agencies
       subscription agencies
                    aging of literatures
                    aging of materials
           computer aided design
           computer aided engineering
           computer aided manufacturing
           computer aided software engineering
               user aids
                    algorithms
                    almanacs
                    alphabetical arrangement
                    alphabetico classed indexes
                    alphabets
                    alternative publications
                    ambiguity
              Anglo American Cataloguing Rules
                    analog data
                    analog systems
        digital to analog conversion
                    analysis of variance
           citation analysis
```

```
            cluster analysis
     co-occurrence analysis
        cocitation analysis
           content analysis
     cost benefit analysis
              data analysis
         discourse analysis
             facet analysis
            factor analysis
    finite element analysis
           Fourier analysis
             image analysis
           lexical analysis
        linguistic analysis
      morphological analysis
       multivariate analysis
           network analysis
          semantic analysis
           subject analysis
         syntactic analysis
           systems analysis
            vector analysis
         work flow analysis
       information analysis centers
                   analytical bibliography
                   anaphora
                   Anglo American Cataloguing Rules
                   animation
                   annotations
                   answer passage retrieval
                   anthropology
                   antonymy
          computer applications
                   approval plans
                   architecture
          computer architectures
                   archival storage
                   archives
                   archivists
                   area studies
             local area networks
      metropolitan area networks
              wide area networks
                   armed forces
                   arrangement
       alphabetical arrangement
   letter by letter arrangement
         systematic arrangement
        word by word arrangement
                   array processors
                   art
          periodical articles
                   artificial intelligence
               fine arts
         performing arts
              legal aspects
       psychological aspects
             social aspects
         collection assessment
              needs assessment
                   assignment indexing
           computer assisted instruction
        information associations
            library associations
       professional associations
```

```
                              associative memory
                              associative relationships
                              associative retrieval
                      quality assurance
                              attitudes
                              audio communications
                              audio interfaces
                      digital audio tapes
                              audiocassettes
                              audiotapes
                              audiotex
                              auditing
                              author abstracts
                              author indexes
                              author-prepared indexes
                              authoring (hypermedia)
                              authority files
                              authors
                              authorship
                              automata
                              automatic abstracting
                              automatic classification
                              automatic extracting
                              automatic indexing
                              automatic...
                              automation
                      library automation
                       office automation
                      current awareness services
                              back end processors
                              banned materials
                              bar codes
                     language barriers
                          pen based computing
                        paper based information systems
                         menu based interfaces
                    knowledge bases
                              basic education
                              batch processing
                              Bayesian functions
                        human behavior
                       search behavior
                         user behavior
                              behavioral sciences
                              benchmarks
                         cost benefit analysis
                        links (between indexing terms)
                              bibliographic access
                              bibliographic citations
                              bibliographic control
                              bibliographic coupling
                              bibliographic databases
                              bibliographic instruction
                              bibliographic records
                              bibliographic utilities
                  cataloging (bibliographic)
                   catalogs (bibliographic)
                              bibliographies
                     national bibliographies
                              bibliography
                   analytical bibliography
                              bibliometrics
                      scatter (bibliometrics)
                              bibliotherapy
                              bilingualism
```

```
                              binderies
                              binding
                              biology
                              biomedical sciences
                              bit-mapped images
                              blanket orders
                   bulletin board systems
                              book collecting
                              book indexes
                              book indexing
                              book reviews
                              book vendors
                   standard book numbers
                              bookmobiles
                              books
                    talking books
                              Boolean logic
                              Boolean searching
                              Bradford's law
                              Braille
                              branch libraries
                              broadband transmission
                              broadcasting
                information brokers
                              browsing
                              budgeting
                              buildings
                    library buildings
                              bulletin board systems
                    service bureaus
                              business
                      query by example
                     letter by letter arrangement
                       word by word arrangement
                              cable television
                    coaxial cable
                              cameras
                        off campus education
                        off campus library services
                              candidate descriptors
                              card catalogs
                      Monte Carlo method
                     common carrier networks
                              cartography
                              case grammar
                              case studies
                              cassette recorders
                              cataloging (bibliographic)
                              cataloging in publication
                              cataloging rules
                computerized cataloging
                 descriptive cataloging
                     minimal cataloging
               retrospective cataloging
                      shared cataloging
                              catalogs (bibliographic)
                        card catalogs
                  classified catalogs
                       union catalogs
              Anglo American Cataloguing Rules
                              categories
                              CD-ROM
                              CD-ROM drives
                              cellular communications
                              censorship
```

```
                    computer centers
       information analysis centers
                       media centers
                             central libraries
                             centralization
                             chain indexing
                             change
                             character sets
                     optical character recognition
                        flow charting
                organization charts
                     spelling checkers
                             chemical information
                             chemical nomenclature
                             chemical structures
                             chemistry
            connection tables (chemistry)
                             children's libraries
                             children's literature
                             children's services
                   integrated circuits
                             circulation (library)
                             citation analysis
                             citation indexes
                             citation order
                             citation searching
              bibliographic citations
                             civil rights
                             claiming (acquisitions)
                 alphabetico classed indexes
                             classification
                             classification schemes
                   automatic classification
              Dewey Decimal Classification
                     faceted classification
                hierarchical classification
        International Patent Classification
        Library of Congress Classification
                    security classification
            Universal Decimal Classification
                             classified catalogs
                             client server systems
                             cluster analysis
                             co-occurrence analysis
                             coauthors
                             coaxial cable
                             cocitation analysis
                         bar codes
                        hash coding
                 superimposed coding
                             cognition
                             cognitive models
                             cognitive science
                             cognitive styles
                        book collecting
                             collection assessment
                             collection development
                             collection management
                        data collection
                             collections
                     library collections
                    personal collections
                     special collections
                   community college libraries
                             colleges and universities
```

```
                        color displays
                        command driven interfaces
                        command languages
              common command language
                        common carrier networks
                        common command language
                        common sense knowledge
                        communications
                        communications patterns
                        communications protocols
                        communications skills
               audio communications
             cellular communications
   computer mediated communications
             digital communications
          electronic communications
       face to face communications
            informal communications
              mobile communications
     multiple access communications
           nonverbal communications
                oral communications
      organizational communications
           satellite communications
               video communications
               voice communications
                        community college libraries
                        community information services
                        community resource files
                        compact disc interactive
                        compact discs
                        compact storage
                        company information
                        comparative librarianship
                        compatibility
                        competition
                        competitive intelligence
                        complexity
                        comprehension
                        compression
                        computational lexicography
                        computational linguistics
                        computer aided design
                        computer aided engineering
                        computer aided manufacturing
                        computer aided software engineering
                        computer applications
                        computer architectures
                        computer assisted instruction
                        computer centers
                        computer conferencing
                        computer crime
                        computer equipment
                        computer graphics
                        computer industry
                        computer integrated manufacturing
                        computer laboratories
                        computer literacy
                        computer mediated communications
                        computer output microform
                        computer peripherals
                        computer programming
                        computer science
                        computer security
                        computer simulation
```

```
                              computer software
                              computer storage
                              computer systems
                              computer vision
                  human computer interfaces
                   mice (computer peripherals)
             trackballs (computer peripherals)
         access control (computer systems)
                 memory (computer)
                 viruses (computer)
                              computerized cataloging
                              computers
             mainframe computers
               optical computers
          optoelectronic computers
              personal computers
        processing units (computers)
                              computing resource management
             distributed computing
               end user computing
                 online computing
             pen based computing
                              concepts
             perception (conceptual)
                              concordances
               computer conferencing
                              confidential records
         Library of Congress Classification
         Library of Congress Subject Headings
                              connection tables (chemistry)
                              connectionist models
                              connectivity
                              conservation of library materials
               indexer consistency
                              consortia
        index language construction
                              consultants
                              consumer information
                              content addressable memory
                              content analysis
                              contents lists
                              context free languages
                              continuing education
                              control systems
          bibliographic control
               quality control
                remote control
            vocabulary control
                access control (computer systems)
                              controlled vocabularies
                  data conversion
              database conversion
      digital to analog conversion
         retrospective conversion
                              cooperation
                              copyright
                              core literature
                              corporate libraries
                              corporate names
                 error correction
                              correspondence
                              correspondence study
                  data corruption
                              cost benefit analysis
                              cost effectiveness
```

111

```
                              cost recovery
                              costs
                     overhead costs
                bibliographic coupling
                              courseware
                              creativity
                     computer crime
                              critical incident method
                              critical path method
                              cross matching
                              cross references
                              crossfile searching
                              cryptography
               organizational culture
                              cumulative indexes
                              currency (in time)
                              current awareness services
                              cybernetics
             information life cycle
                              data
                              data analysis
                              data collection
                              data conversion
                              data corruption
                              data dictionaries
                              data distribution
                              data entry
                              data formats
                              data models
                              data processing
                              data reduction
                              data security
                              data structures
                              data transmission
                       analog data
              machine readable data
                      numeric data
                     personal data
                  transborder data flow
                   electronic data interchange
                      objects (data structures)
                     abstract data types
                              database conversion
                              database design
                              database indexing
                              database leasing
                              database machines
                              database maintenance
                              database management systems
                              database models
                              database producers
                              databases
                bibliographic databases
                    deductive databases
                  distributed databases
                         fact databases
                    full text databases
                        image databases
             nonbibliographic databases
                      numeric databases
               object oriented databases
                       online databases
                   relational databases
                              decentralization
                 Dewey Decimal Classification
```

```
              Universal Decimal Classification
                        decision making
                        decision support systems
                        decision theory
                  group decision support systems
                        decoding
                        decryption
                        dedicated systems
                        deductive databases
                        default values
               document delivery
                        demographics
                   high density storage
                  legal deposit
                        depository libraries
                        depth (indexing)
                        derivative indexing
                        descriptive cataloging
                        descriptors
              candidate descriptors
                        deselection
                        design
         computer aided design
               database design
                  forms design
                 screen design
                systems design
                        desktop metaphor
                        desktop publishing
              duplicate detection
                  error detection
             collection development
          research and development
                systems development
               pointing devices
                        Dewey Decimal Classification
                        diacriticals
                        dictionaries
                   data dictionaries
             individual differences
                        diffusion of innovation
                        digests
                        digital audio tapes
                        digital communications
                        digital to analog conversion
                        digital video interactive
                        digitization
                        digitized images
                        directories
                        disabled persons
               learning disabled persons
                reading disabled persons
                        disambiguation
                        disasters
                compact disc interactive
                        disclosure
                        discourse analysis
                        discourse generation
                compact discs
       erasable optical discs
              floptical discs
                optical discs
                   WORM discs
                        disk drives
                        disks
```

```
                       floppy disks
                         hard disks
                     magnetic disks
             magneto-optical disks
                     video display terminals
                             displays
                       color displays
             high resolution displays
                   thesaurus displays
                 information dissemination
                             dissertations
                             distance learning
                             distributed computing
                             distributed databases
                        data distribution
                             document access
                             document delivery
                             document handling
                             document retrieval
                             document surrogates
                             documentary languages
                             documentation
                 retention of documents
                             domain knowledge
                      public domain software
                             downloading
                             DRAM
                             DRAW
                 engineering drawings
                     command driven interfaces
                      CD-ROM drives
                        disk drives
                             duplicate detection
                             duplicate records
                             durability
                             dynamic systems
                             early adopters
                             earth sciences
                             ecology
                             econometrics
                             economics
                             economics of information
           information sector (economy)
                             editing
                             editors
                        text editors
                             education
                       adult education
                       basic education
                  continuing education
                        home education
         information science education
                     library education
                  off campus education
    National Research and Education Network
                             educational technology
                             effectiveness
                        cost effectiveness
                   retrieval effectiveness
                             efficiency
                             electronic communications
                             electronic data interchange
                             electronic filing
                             electronic funds transfer systems
                             electronic journals
```

```
                              electronic mail
                              electronic publications
                              electronic publishing
                       finite element analysis
                              empirical studies
                              employees
                              employment
                              encoding
                              encryption
                              encyclopedias
                              end user computing
                              end user searching
                              end users
                         back end processors
                        front ends
                              engineering
                              engineering drawings
             computer aided engineering
    computer aided software engineering
                   knowledge engineering
                    software engineering
                              English language
                        image enhancement
                              entrepreneurs
                              entrepreneurship
                              entries
                              entropy (information)
                              entry vocabularies
                         data entry
               organizational environment
                              ephemera
                     computer equipment
                        input equipment
                      library equipment
                      optical equipment
                       output equipment
           telecommunications equipment
                     printers (equipment)
                              equivalence relationships
                              erasable optical discs
                              ergonomics
                              erotic materials
                              error correction
                              error detection
                              error messages
                              error rates
                              errors
                typographical errors
                              ethics
                              etymology
                              evaluation
                              exact match searching
                     query by example
                  gifts and exchanges
                              executive information systems
                              exhaustivity (indexing)
                        query expansion
                         user expectations
                              experiments
                              expert systems
                      subject experts
                              explanation
                  information explosion
                              extracting
                    automatic extracting
```

```
            feature extraction
                    face to face communications
            face to face communications
                    facet analysis
                    faceted classification
                    facsimile transmission
                    fact databases
                    fact retrieval systems
                    factor analysis
              human factors
                    fallout
                    fault tolerance
                    feature extraction
                    feedback
        look and feel
                    fees for service
                    fiber optics
                    fiction
                    file integrity
                    file servers
                    file structures
                    file transfers
       hierarchical file structures
                    files
          authority files
  community resource files
     human resource files
          inverted files
          personal files
          vertical files
         electronic filing
              form filling
                    films
       photographic films
                    filmstrips
        information filtering
                    finance
                    financial management
                    fine arts
                    finite element analysis
                    flexible manufacturing systems
                    floppy disks
                    floptical discs
                    flow charting
        information flow
    transborder data flow
              work flow analysis
                    focus groups
                    font learning
             armed forces
                    forecasting
                    foreign language materials
                    foreign languages
                    form filling
              data formats
       interchange formats
              MARC formats
                    formatting
                    forms design
             query formulation
                    Fourier analysis
                    free text searching
           context free languages
                    freedom of information
                    freedom to read
```

116

```
             academic freedom
         intellectual freedom
                      frequency of use
                 word frequency
                      friends of libraries
                      front ends
                      full text databases
                      full text searching
             Bayesian functions
           electronic funds transfer systems
                      fuzzy retrieval systems
                      fuzzy set theory
                      game theory
                video games
                      gatekeepers
                      gateways
                      gender
                      genealogy
                      generalization
            discourse generation
             sentence generation
                      generic posting
                      genomes
                      genus species relationships
                      geographic information systems
                      geography
                      gifts and exchanges
                      goals
                      government agencies
                      government libraries
                      government publications
                 case grammar
                      grammars
                      grants
                      graph processing
                      graph theory
              mapping (graphic representation)
                      graphical thesauri
                      graphical user interfaces
                      graphics
             computer graphics
                      graphs
                      grey literature
                      group decision support systems
                      group work
                focus groups
                      groupware
                      growth
                      handbooks
             document handling
                      hard disks
                      hash coding
                      HDTV
              subject heading lists
                      headings
Library of Congress Subject Headings
               Sears Subject Headings
              subject headings
                      hedges (online searching)
                      help systems
                      heuristics
                      hierarchical classification
                      hierarchical file structures
                      hierarchical models
                      hierarchical relationships
```

```
                             hierarchies
                             high density storage
                             high level languages
                             high resolution displays
                             history
                        oral history
                             holographic memory
                             holography
                             home education
                             home information services
                  working at home
                             homography
                             Hough transformation
                             human behavior
                             human computer interfaces
                             human factors
                             human information sources
                             human resource files
                             human resource management
                  memory (human)
                             humanities
                             hybrid systems
                             hypercube systems
                             hypermedia
                authoring (hypermedia)
                             hypertext
                    links (hypertext)
                             icons
                             identification
                             identifiers
                             ideographs
                             idioms
                             illustrations
                             image analysis
                             image databases
                             image enhancement
                             image information systems
                             image processing
                             image retrieval
                             image servers
                             images
               bit-mapped images
                digitized images
                             imaging
      magnetic resonance imaging
              technology impact
                 critical incident method
                             index language construction
                             index languages
                             index terms
                             indexer consistency
                             indexes (information retrieval)
     alphabetico classed indexes
                  author indexes
          author-prepared indexes
                    book indexes
                citation indexes
              cumulative indexes
                 keyword indexes
                    KWIC indexes
                    KWOC indexes
               periodical indexes
                permuted indexes
                 subject indexes
                             indexing
```

```
             assignment indexing
              automatic indexing
                   book indexing
                  chain indexing
               database indexing
             derivative indexing
                 manual indexing
     multilingual subject indexing
                   name indexing
               periodical indexing
          postcoordinate indexing
           precoordinate indexing
            probabilistic indexing
                 string indexing
                subject indexing
        abstracting and indexing services
          links (between indexing terms)
                  depth (indexing)
           exhaustivity (indexing)
            specificity (indexing)
                        indicators (values)
                   role indicators
                        individual differences
               computer industry
            information industry
                 online industry
               software industry
      telecommunications industry
                        inference
                        infometrics
                        informal communications
                        informatics
                medical informatics
                 museum informatics
                        information
                        information access
                        information analysis centers
                        information associations
                        information brokers
                        information dissemination
                        information explosion
                        information filtering
                        information flow
                        information industry
                        information infrastructure
                        information life cycle
                        information literacy
                        information models
                        information needs
                        information overload
                        information policy
                        information processing
                        information production
                        information professionals
                        information representations
                        information resources management
                        information retrieval
                        information retrieval systems
                        information science
                        information science education
                        information scientists
                        information sector (economy)
                        information seeking
                        information services
                        information society
```

119

```
                                    information sources
                                    information technology
                                    information theory
                                    information transfer
                                    information use
                                    information utilities
                                    information workers
                         chemical information
                          company information
                         consumer information
                     economics of information
                       freedom of information
                  organization of information
                           public information
        scientific and technical information
                          indexes (information retrieval)
                            noise (information retrieval)
                      community information services
                             home information services
                            human information sources
                        executive information systems
                       geographic information systems
                            image information systems
                       management information systems
                      paper based information systems
                          entropy (information)
            information infrastructure
                                    innovation
                     diffusion of innovation
                                    input equipment
                                    institutional libraries
                   bibliographic instruction
               computer assisted instruction
                                    instrumentation
                                    integrated circuits
                                    integrated library systems
                                    integrated systems
                         computer integrated manufacturing
                          systems integration
                             file integrity
                                    intellectual freedom
                                    intellectual property
                                    intelligence
                       artificial intelligence
                      competitive intelligence
                                    intelligent interfaces
                                    interactive systems
                      compact disc interactive
                      digital video interactive
                                    interchange formats
                electronic data interchange
                                    interdisciplinarity
                             audio interfaces
                    command driven interfaces
                     graphical user interfaces
                     human computer interfaces
                        intelligent interfaces
                        menu based interfaces
                  natural language interfaces
                      touch screen interfaces
                                    interlibrary loans
                                    international librarianship
                                    International Patent Classification
                                    Internet
                         presearch interviews
```

120

```
          reference interviews
                    inventory
                    inverted files
                    ISDN
              known item searching
                    jargon
                    journals
         electronic journals
                    joysticks
          relevance judgments
                    jukeboxes
                    keyboards
                    keyword indexes
                    keyword searching
                    keywords
                    knowledge
                    knowledge acquisition
                    knowledge bases
                    knowledge engineering
                    knowledge representation
       common sense knowledge
             domain knowledge
             system knowledge
               task knowledge
                    known item searching
                    KWIC indexes
                    KWOC indexes
                    labor unions
           computer laboratories
                    language barriers
     common command language
            English language
              index language construction
            natural language interfaces
            foreign language materials
            natural language processing
            natural language searching
            natural language understanding
                    languages
            command languages
       context free languages
        documentary languages
            foreign languages
         high level languages
              index languages
             markup languages
        programming languages
              query languages
   structured query languages
          switching languages
                    large print materials
                    lasers
                    law
          Bradford's law
            Lotka's law
             Zipf's law
                    leadership
              loose leaf services
                    learning
                    learning disabled persons
           distance learning
               font learning
           lifelong learning
            machine learning
         perceptual learning
```

121

```
                  database leasing
                           legal aspects
                           legal deposit
                           legibility
                    public lending right
                           letter by letter arrangement
            letter by letter arrangement
                      high level languages
                           lexical analysis
                           lexicography
             computational lexicography
                           liability
                           librarians
                 reference librarians
                           librarianship
               comparative librarianship
             international librarianship
                           libraries
                  academic libraries
                    branch libraries
                   central libraries
                children's libraries
        community college libraries
                 corporate libraries
                depository libraries
                friends of libraries
               government libraries
             institutional libraries
                    mobile libraries
                  national libraries
              Presidential libraries
                    public libraries
                  research libraries
                     small libraries
                   special libraries
                     state libraries
                   virtual libraries
        technical services (libraries)
                           library access
                           library associations
                           library automation
                           library buildings
                           library collections
                           library education
                           library equipment
                           library management
                           library materials
                           library networks
                           Library of Congress Classification
                           Library of Congress Subject Headings
                           library personnel
                           library programs
                           library schools
                           library security systems
                           library services
                           library shelving
                           library skills
                           library suppliers
                           library supplies
                           library surveys
                           library users
                           library weeks
                     state library agencies
          conservation of library materials
          preservation of library materials
```

```
      paraprofessional library personnel
            off campus library services
            integrated library systems
               circulation (library)
      outreach services (library)
               information life cycle
                             lifelong learning
                             light pens
                             linear programming
                             linguistic analysis
                             linguistics
             computational linguistics
                             links (between indexing terms)
                             links (hypertext)
                    contents lists
             subject heading lists
                             listservs
                             literacy
                    computer literacy
                 information literacy
                             literary warrant
                             literature
                             literature reviews
                children's literature
                        core literature
                        grey literature
                     primary literature
                young adult literature
                    aging of literatures
                             litigation support
                interlibrary loans
                             local area networks
                    physical location
                             locators
                             logic
                             logic programming
                     Boolean logic
                   predicate logic
               propositional logic
                             logical skills
                             long term memory
                             look and feel
                             loose leaf services
                             Lotka's law
                             LSI
                             machine learning
                             machine readable data
                             machine translation
                    database machines
                             magnetic disks
                             magnetic media
                             magnetic recording
                             magnetic resonance imaging
                             magnetic tapes
                             magneto-optical disks
                  electronic mail
                       voice mail
                             mainframe computers
                             maintainability
                             maintenance
                    database maintenance
                   thesaurus maintenance
                    decision making
                             management
                             management information systems
```

123

```
                 collection management
        computing resource management
                  financial management
             human resource management
        information resources management
                    library management
                    records management
          database management systems
                           managers
                   records managers
                           manual indexing
          computer aided manufacturing
     computer integrated manufacturing
                  flexible manufacturing systems
                           manuscripts
                           mapping (graphic representation)
                           mapping (sets)
                           maps
                           MARC formats
                           MARC records
                           marginalia
                           marketing
                           Markov models
                           markup languages
                           mass media
                     exact match searching
                     cross matching
                 aging of materials
                    banned materials
      conservation of library materials
                    erotic materials
         foreign language materials
               large print materials
                   library materials
                   overdue materials
                    popular materials
              pornographic materials
       preservation of library materials
                     print materials
                      rare materials
           ready reference materials
                 reference materials
                    visual materials
          acquisitions (of materials)
                  ordering (materials)
              selection (of materials)
                   storage (materials)
                           mathematical methods
                           mathematical models
                           mathematics
                           matrices
                           measurement
                           media
                           media centers
                           media specialists
                  magnetic media
                      mass media
                  nonprint media
                   optical media
                  computer mediated communications
                           medical informatics
                           medical records
                           medicine
                           meetings
                           memory (computer)
```

```
                        memory (human)
            associative memory
    content addressable memory
            holographic memory
              long term memory
          random access memory
            read only memory
            short term memory
                 virtual memory
                  visual memory
                        mental processes
                        menu based interfaces
                        message systems
                  error messages
                desktop metaphor
                        metaphors
      critical incident method
         critical path method
            Monte Carlo method
           mathematical methods
               research methods
             statistical methods
                        metropolitan area networks
                        mice (computer peripherals)
                        microcomputers
                        microfiche
                        microfilm
         computer output microform
                        microforms
                        microprocessors
                        microprograms
                        micropublishing
                        microthesauri
                        minicomputers
                        minimal cataloging
                        mission oriented research
                        mobile communications
                        mobile libraries
                        models
               cognitive models
          connectionist models
                  data models
              database models
           hierarchical models
            information models
                 Markov models
           mathematical models
              predictive models
               relational models
               stochastic models
                   user models
          vector space models
                        modems
                        modifiers
                        modularity
                        monitoring
                        monographs
                        Monte Carlo method
                        morphological analysis
                        motion video
                        motivation
                        moving
                        multilingual subject indexing
                        multilingual thesauri
                        multimedia
```

```
                                    multiple access communications
                                    multiplexing
                                    multiprocessing
                                    multiprocessors
                                    multitasking
                                    multivariate analysis
                                    museum informatics
                                    museums
                                    music
                                    name indexing
                      corporate names
                       personal names
                         proper names
                                    national bibliographies
                                    national libraries
                                    National Research and Education Network
                                    natural language interfaces
                                    natural language processing
                                    natural language searching
                                    natural language understanding
                                    natural sciences
                                    navigation
                                    needs assessment
                   information needs
                                    negotiation
                                    network analysis
    National Research and Education Network
                        traffic (network)
                       personal networking
                                    networks
               common carrier networks
                       library networks
                    local area networks
             metropolitan area networks
                        neural networks
                      semantic networks
              telecommunications networks
                      wide area networks
                                    neural networks
                                    news
                                    newsletters
                                    newspapers
                                    newswire services
                                    nodes
                                    noise (acoustic)
                                    noise (information retrieval)
                       chemical nomenclature
                                    nonbibliographic databases
                                    nonfiction
                                    nonlinear programming
                                    nonprint media
                                    nonroman scripts
                                    nonverbal communications
                                    normalization
                                    notation
                                    notation synthesis
                           scope notes
                                    novice users
                   standard book numbers
                 standard serial numbers
                                    numeric data
                                    numeric databases
                                    object oriented databases
                                    object oriented programming
                                    object recognition
```

```
                            objects (data structures)
               physical objects
                            obsolescence
                            off campus education
                            off campus library services
                            office automation
                            online computing
                            online databases
                            online industry
                            online searchers
                            online searching
                 hedges (online searching)
                            online...
                    read only memory
                            OPACs
                            operating systems
                            operations research
                            optical character recognition
                            optical computers
                            optical discs
                            optical equipment
                            optical media
                            optical recognition
                            optical recording
                            optical tape
               erasable optical discs
                  fiber optics
                            optimization
                            optoelectronic computers
                            oral communications
                            oral history
               citation order
                            ordering (materials)
                blanket orders
               standing orders
                            organization charts
                            organization of information
                            organization theory
                            organizational communications
                            organizational culture
                            organizational environment
                            organizations
                 object oriented databases
                 object oriented programming
                mission oriented research
                            out of print publications
                            output equipment
                            output reformatting
               computer output microform
                            outreach services (library)
                            overdue materials
                            overhead costs
                            overlap
            information overload
                            packet switching
                            paper
                            paper based information systems
                            paperbacks
                            paradigms
                            parallel processing
                            parallel processors
                            paraprofessional library personnel
                            part whole relationships
                            participative problem solving
                 answer passage retrieval
```

```
          International Patent Classification
                       patents
             critical path method
             problem patrons
                       pattern recognition
      communications patterns
                       pay per view television
                       pen based computing
               light pens
                 pay per view television
                       perception (conceptual)
                       perception (sensory)
                       perceptual learning
                       performance
                       performing arts
                       periodical articles
                       periodical indexes
                       periodical indexing
                       periodicals
            computer peripherals
    mice (computer peripherals)
trackballs (computer peripherals)
                       permanence
                       permuted indexes
                       personal collections
                       personal computers
                       personal data
                       personal files
                       personal names
                       personal networking
             library personnel
paraprofessional library personnel
            disabled persons
    learning disabled persons
     reading disabled persons
                       pharmacology
                       philosophy
                       phonetics
                       photocopiers
                       photocopying
                       photogrammetry
                       photographic films
                       photographs
                       phrases
                       physical location
                       physical objects
                       physical sciences
                       physicians
                       physics
                       planning
           strategic planning
            approval plans
                       poetry
                       pointing devices
              access points
         information policy
              public policy
                       political science
                       politics
                       popular materials
                       pornographic materials
                       postcoordinate indexing
             generic posting
                       pragmatics
                       PRECIS
```

```
                          precision
                          precoordinate indexing
                          predicate logic
                          predictive models
                          preprints
                          presearch interviews
                          preservation of library materials
                          Presidential libraries
                    small presses
                          pricing
                          primary literature
                          print materials
                    large print materials
                   out of print publications
                          printers (equipment)
                          printing
                          privacy
                          private sector
                          probabilistic indexing
                          probabilistic retrieval
                          probability
                          problem patrons
                          problem solving
            participative problem solving
                   mental processes
               stochastic processes
                          processing units (computers)
                    batch processing
                     data processing
                    graph processing
                    image processing
              information processing
         natural language processing
                 parallel processing
                    query processing
                real time processing
                   signal processing
                     text processing
                     word processing
                    array processors
                 back end processors
                 parallel processors
                 database producers
              information production
                          productivity
                          professional associations
              information professionals
                          programming languages
                 computer programming
                   linear programming
                    logic programming
                nonlinear programming
           object oriented programming
                  library programs
                          promotion
                          proofreading
                          proper names
             intellectual property
                          propositional logic
           communications protocols
                          prototyping
                          proximity searching
                          psychological aspects
                          psychology
                   social psychology
```

129

```
                                  psychometrics
                                  public domain software
                                  public information
                                  public lending right
                                  public libraries
                                  public policy
                                  public records
                                  public relations
                                  public sector
                   cataloging in publication
                                  publications
                    alternative publications
                     electronic publications
                     government publications
                   out of print publications
                                  publishers
                                  publishing
                        desktop publishing
                     electronic publishing
                      scholarly publishing
                                  qualifiers
                                  qualitative research
                                  quality
                                  quality assurance
                                  quality control
                                  quasi-synonymous relationships
                                  query by example
                                  query expansion
                                  query formulation
                                  query languages
                                  query processing
                                  query refinement
                     structured query languages
                                  queuing
                                  radiation
                                  radio
                                  random access memory
                                  range searching
                       relevance ranking
                                  rare materials
                           error rates
                                  read only memory
                      freedom to read
                         machine readable data
                                  reader services
                                  reading
                                  reading disabled persons
                                  ready reference materials
                                  real time processing
                                  realia
                         virtual reality
                                  reasoning
                                  recall
                          object recognition
          optical character recognition
                         optical recognition
                         pattern recognition
                          speech recognition
                            word recognition
                        cassette recorders
                            tape recorders
                           video recorders
                   videocassette recorders
                                  recording
                        magnetic recording
```

```
                   optical recording
                     sound recordings
                     video recordings
                           records
                           records management
                           records managers
            administrative records
            admissibility of records
             bibliographic records
              confidential records
                 duplicate records
                      MARC records
                   medical records
                    public records
                      cost recovery
                      data reduction
                           refereeing
                           reference interviews
                           reference librarians
                           reference materials
                           reference retrieval systems
                           reference services
                           reference skills
                     ready reference materials
                     cross references
                     query refinement
                    output reformatting
                           relational databases
                           relational models
                    public relations
                associative relationships
                equivalence relationships
             genus species relationships
               hierarchical relationships
                part whole relationships
          quasi-synonymous relationships
                  semantic relationships
                           relevance
                           relevance judgments
                           relevance ranking
                           reliability
                           remote access
                           remote control
                           remote sensing
                 technical reports
                 knowledge representation
          mapping (graphic representation)
               information representations
                           research and development
                           research libraries
                           research methods
           mission oriented research
                operations research
                qualitative research
                  National Research and Education Network
                      high resolution displays
                  magnetic resonance imaging
                           resource sharing
                 community resource files
                     human resource files
                 computing resource management
                     human resource management
                 access to resources
               information resources management
                           response time
```

131

```
                                        restoration
                                        retention of documents
                                        retrieval effectiveness
                                        retrieval software
                       answer passage retrieval
                          associative retrieval
                             document retrieval
                                image retrieval
                          information retrieval
                        probabilistic retrieval
                                 fact retrieval systems
                                fuzzy retrieval systems
                          information retrieval systems
                            reference retrieval systems
              indexes (information retrieval)
                noise (information retrieval)
                                        retrospective cataloging
                                        retrospective conversion
                                        reviewing
                                        reviews
                                 book reviews
                           literature reviews
                       public lending right
                                civil rights
                                        RISC
                                        robotics
                                        robots
                                        role indicators
                                        romanization
                                        royalties
        Anglo American Cataloguing Rules
                           cataloging rules
                                        sampling
                                        satellite communications
                                 user satisfaction
                                        scanners
                                        scanning
                                        scatter (bibliometrics)
                                        scheduling
                       classification schemes
                                        scholarly publishing
                              library schools
                            cognitive science
                             computer science
                          information science
                            political science
                          information science education
                           behavioral sciences
                            biomedical sciences
                                earth sciences
                              natural sciences
                             physical sciences
                               social sciences
                                        scientific and technical information
                          information scientists
                                        scientometrics
                                        scope notes
                                        screen design
                                touch screen interfaces
                             nonroman scripts
                                        SDI services
                                        search behavior
                                        search services
                                        search strategies
                                        search terms
```

```
                              search time
                    online searchers
                           searching
                   Boolean searching
                  citation searching
                 crossfile searching
                  end user searching
               exact match searching
                 free text searching
                 full text searching
                   keyword searching
                known item searching
          natural language searching
                    online searching
                 proximity searching
                     range searching
                sequential searching
                    string searching
                   subject searching
          hedges (online searching)
                           Sears Subject Headings
                     trade secrets
                   private sector
                    public sector
               information sector (economy)
                           security
                           security classification
                  computer security
                      data security
                   library security systems
               information seeking
                           selection (of materials)
                           semantic analysis
                           semantic networks
                           semantic relationships
                           semantics
                           semiotics
                    common sense knowledge
                    remote sensing
                           sensors
               perception (sensory)
                           sentence generation
                           sentences
                      sort sequences
                           sequential searching
                           serendipity
                  standard serial numbers
                           serials
                           series
                    client server systems
                      file servers
                     image servers
                           service bureaus
                  fees for service
      abstracting and indexing services
               children's services
     community information services
         current awareness services
          home information services
               information services
                   library services
                 loose leaf services
                   newswire services
        off campus library services
                    reader services
```

133

```
             reference services
                   SDI services
                search services
          young adult services
            technical services (libraries)
             outreach services (library)
                       set theory
                 fuzzy set theory
            character sets
              mapping (sets)
                       shared cataloging
                       shareware
              resource sharing
               library shelving
                       short term memory
                       signal processing
                       similarity
                       simulation
              computer simulation
        communications skills
               library skills
               logical skills
             reference skills
                       slides
                       small libraries
                       small presses
                       social aspects
                       social psychology
                       social sciences
           information society
                       socioeconomics
                       sociograms
                       sociology
                       sociometrics
                       software engineering
                       software industry
              computer software
         public domain software
             retrieval software
               utility software
         computer aided software engineering
  participative problem solving
               problem solving
                       sort sequences
                       sorting
                       sound
                       sound recordings
      human information sources
            information sources
                vector space models
                       special collections
                       special libraries
                 media specialists
                 genus species relationships
                       specificity (indexing)
                       speech
                       speech recognition
                       speech synthesis
           transmission speed
                       spelling checkers
                       spreading activation
                       spreadsheets
                       standard book numbers
                       standard serial numbers
                       standardization
```

```
                          standards
                          standing orders
                          state libraries
                          state library agencies
                          statistical methods
                          stemming
                          stochastic models
                          stochastic processes
                          stoplists
                          storage (materials)
              archival storage
               compact storage
              computer storage
         high density storage
                          storytelling
                          strategic planning
                search strategies
                          string indexing
                          string searching
                          structured query languages
              chemical structures
                  data structures
                  file structures
     hierarchical file structures
              syndetic structures
                  tree structures
         objects (data structures)
                          students
                  area studies
                  case studies
             empirical studies
                 usage studies
                  user studies
         correspondence study
             cognitive styles
                          subject access
                          subject analysis
                          subject experts
                          subject heading lists
                          subject headings
                          subject indexes
                          subject indexing
                          subject searching
   Library of Congress Subject Headings
                 Sears Subject Headings
           multilingual subject indexing
                          subscription agencies
                          subscriptions
                          suffixes
                          summarization
                          supercomputers
                          superimposed coding
                          superminicomputers
               library suppliers
               library supplies
            litigation support
              decision support systems
        group decision support systems
              document surrogates
                          surveys
               library surveys
                          switching languages
                packet switching
                          symbols
                          syndetic structures
```

```
                                 syntactic analysis
                                 syntactics
                        notation synthesis
                          speech synthesis
                                 system knowledge
                                 systematic arrangement
                                 systems analysis
                                 systems design
                                 systems development
                                 systems integration
                          analog systems
                  bulletin board systems
                   client server systems
                        computer systems
                         control systems
             database management systems
                decision support systems
                       dedicated systems
                         dynamic systems
      electronic funds transfer systems
           executive information systems
                          expert systems
                  fact retrieval systems
          flexible manufacturing systems
                 fuzzy retrieval systems
          geographic information systems
          group decision support systems
                            help systems
                          hybrid systems
                       hypercube systems
              image information systems
           information retrieval systems
              integrated library systems
                      integrated systems
                     interactive systems
                library security systems
          management information systems
                         message systems
                       operating systems
          paper based information systems
              reference retrieval systems
                         turnkey systems
                         writing systems
         access control (computer systems)
                      connection tables (chemistry)
                                 talking books
                                 tape recorders
                         optical tape
                   digital audio tapes
                        magnetic tapes
                                 task knowledge
                                 taxonomy
                                 technical reports
                                 technical services (libraries)
                                 technical writing
                  scientific and technical information
                                 technology impact
                                 technology transfer
                     educational technology
                     information technology
                                 telecommunications
                                 telecommunications equipment
                                 telecommunications industry
                                 telecommunications networks
                                 telecommuting
```

```
                                  teleconferencing
                          video teleconferencing
                                  telegraphy
                                  telemarketing
                                  telemetry
                                  telephones
                                  telerobotics
                                  teleshopping
                                  teletext
                                  television
                          cable television
                  pay per view television
                           long term memory
                          short term memory
                  video display terminals
                                  terminology
                                  terms
                          index terms
                         search terms
                            top terms
       links (between indexing terms)
                                  testing
                                  text editors
                                  text processing
                           full text databases
                           free text searching
                           full text searching
                                  textbooks
                       decision theory
                      fuzzy set theory
                           game theory
                          graph theory
                    information theory
                    organization theory
                            set theory
                                  thesauri
                      graphical thesauri
                   multilingual thesauri
                                  thesaurofacet
                                  thesaurus displays
                                  thesaurus maintenance
                       response time
                         search time
                           real time processing
                   currency (in time)
                                  titles
                          fault tolerance
                                  tomography
                                  top terms
                                  touch screen interfaces
                                  trackballs (computer peripherals)
                                  trade secrets
                                  trademarks
                                  traffic (network)
                                  training
                           user training
                                  transborder data flow
                    information transfer
                     technology transfer
              electronic funds transfer systems
                           file transfers
                          Hough transformation
                                  translation
                        machine translation
                                  translators
```

```
                                   transliteration
                                   transmission speed
                        broadband transmission
                             data transmission
                        facsimile transmission
                            voice transmission
                                   transputers
                                   tree structures
                                   truncation
                                   turnkey systems
                                   tutorials
                   abstract data types
                                   typographical errors
                                   typography
                                   uncertainty
                natural language understanding
                                   union catalogs
                            labor unions
                       processing units (computers)
                                   Universal Decimal Classification
                     colleges and universities
                                   updating
                                   uploading
                                   usability
                                   usage studies
                     frequency of use
                      information use
                                   user aids
                                   user behavior
                                   user expectations
                                   user models
                                   user satisfaction
                                   user studies
                                   user training
                             end user computing
                        graphical user interfaces
                             end user searching
                                   users
                             end users
                          library users
                           novice users
                    bibliographic utilities
                      information utilities
                                   utility
                                   utility software
                                   validation
                                   value added
                          default values
                       indicators (values)
                      analysis of variance
                                   vector analysis
                                   vector space models
                                   vendors
                             book vendors
                                   verification
                                   vertical files
                                   video communications
                                   video display terminals
                                   video games
                                   video recorders
                                   video recordings
                                   video teleconferencing
                           motion video
                          digital video interactive
                                   videocassette recorders
```

```
                         videocassettes
                         videodiscs
                         videotelephones
                         videotex
              pay per view television
                         virtual libraries
                         virtual memory
                         virtual reality
                         viruses (computer)
                         vision
         computer vision
                         visual materials
                         visual memory
                         visualization
                         VLSI
       controlled vocabularies
            entry vocabularies
                         vocabulary control
                         voice communications
                         voice mail
                         voice transmission
                         volunteers
          literary warrant
           library weeks
                         weighting
             part whole relationships
                         wide area networks
                         word by word arrangement
                         word frequency
                         word processing
                         word recognition
          word by word arrangement
                         words
                         work flow analysis
            group work
      information workers
                         working at home
                         workshops
                         workstations
                         WORM discs
                         writing systems
        technical writing
                         WYSIWYG
                         yearbooks
                         young adult literature
                         young adult services
                         Zipf's law
```

NOTES

NOTES

NOTES

NOTES

NOTES

NOTES

NOTES

NOTES

NOTES

NOTES

MB94-064
VOCAB